POWER MAD!

A Book of
DERANGED
Dictators

Karl Shaw

MICHAEL O'MARA BOOKS LIMITED

First published in 2004 by
Michael O'Mara Books Limited
9 Lion Yard, Tremadoc Road
London sw4 7nq

A CIP catalogue record for this book is available
from the British Library

ISBN 1-84317-106-6

1 3 5 7 9 10 8 6 4 2

Designed and typeset by Martin Bristow

Printed and bound in Great Britain by Cox & Wyman,
Reading, Berks

www.mombooks.com

Contents

CHAPTER 1
Psychopaths

Idi Amin sold doughnuts by the roadside before enlisting as a private in the King's African Rifles of the British colonial army in Uganda. A popular regimental sportsman, he was always the first to jump to attention and salute flag and monarch. To most of the British officers he was 'a splendid chap, though a bit short of grey matter'. A British diplomat in Uganda concurred; Amin was 'virtually bone from the neck up and needs things explained in words of one letter'. When Amin became ruler of Uganda in 1971, the occasion passed by with barely a murmur of dissent from the international community, which believed him to be semi-literate, stupid and arrogant – but harmless. It didn't occur to them that Amin was also dangerously insane until, in the interests of better relations with Britain, he volunteered to marry Princess Anne.

The court of the nineteenth-century Haitian dictator Faustin Soulouque (the self-styled Emperor Faustin I) was the butt of international caricaturists. Faustin himself was crudely lampooned by the *New York Herald*, among others, as 'the nigger Billy Bowlegs'. In his first month in charge the new emperor created 4 princes, 59 dukes, 2 marquises, 90 counts, 215 barons and 30 chevaliers – a total of 400 titled persons. Faustin established a secret police force, known as the zinglins, to keep dissenters in line, and took part in cannibalistic rites, drinking the blood of his late rivals and keeping their skulls on his desk to use as drinking cups. Faustin once had a suspected enemy called Similien arrested and shackled to a dungeon wall. Later, a report came to Faustin that the man's legs were turning gangrenous from the pressure of his fettles. Faustin sent word back: 'Tell him not to worry. When his legs drop off, I'll chain him by the neck.'

During Christmas celebrations in 1975, the president of Equatorial Guinea, Macias Nguema, ordered his army to shoot 150 political opponents in the Malabo football stadium as loudspeakers played Mary Hopkin's 'Those Were The Days'.

At an Organization of African Unity summit meeting in 1975, Idi Amin entertained his fellow African presidents by demonstrating how to suffocate a person with a handkerchief.

The Dominican Republic's longest serving president Rafael Trujillo was a torturer par excellence, in whose name a variety of methods were employed, including slow-shocking electric chairs, an electrified rod known as 'the cane' (especially effective on genitals), nail extractors, whips, tanks of blood-sucking leeches and 'the octopus', a multi-armed electrical appliance strapped to the head. Trujillo's most respected torturer, however, was a dwarf known as Snowball, who specialized in biting off men's genitals.

Paraguayan dictator Alfredo Stroessner employed a security chief, the tasteful torturer Pastor Coronel, who decorated the walls of his torture chambers with swastikas and pictures of Hitler, Mussolini and General Franco. He also introduced classical music to his 'sessions', to drown out the screams of his victims. Coronel once had the Secretary of the Paraguayan Communist Party torn apart with a chainsaw, to the accompaniment of a polka. The entire proceedings were relayed to Stroessner down the telephone, to ensure that he missed none of the details.

When Idi Amin came to power in Uganda in 1971, Britain sent out a Foreign Office minister, Lord Boyd, to congratulate him. Amin requested a signed portrait of the Queen and a royal visit as soon as possible; he assured Boyd that he had already written Her Majesty 'a very nice letter'. In July 1972 Amin got his wish and went to Buckingham Palace to have lunch with the Queen and her husband, the Duke of Edinburgh, whom he addressed throughout as 'Mr Philip'. Affronted that he was never asked back, Amin wrote to the Queen again three years later: 'I would like you to arrange for me to visit Scotland, Ireland and Wales to meet the heads of revolutionary movements fighting against your imperialist oppression.'

Adolf Hitler was prone to temper tantrums that became worse as the war went on, prompting his subordinates to nickname him 'carpet biter'. His personal physician Dr Theodor Morell recorded that the Führer would often turn white, his jaws tightly clenched and his eyes dilated; a sign for everyone in his entourage to panic because the fits were always followed by an order to dismiss or execute someone. Hitler's mood swings were exacerbated by a variety of minor ailments, including stomach cramps and chronic insomnia, which Morell treated with a regimen of twenty-eight separate medications, including some mercury–lead compounds known to cause mental deterioration, and Dr Köster's anti-gas pills, a mysterious mixture of strychnine and belladonna. Morell also prescribed 'golden' tablets containing huge amounts of caffeine and the highly addictive amphetamine pervitin, large doses of which are known to cause disorientation, hallucination, convulsion and coma. In September 1940 Hitler threatened to bomb England with a million kilograms of explosives. He later amended the figure to 400,000 kilograms because the original quantity, arrived at while under the influence of Morell's pills, on reflection struck him as rather excessive. The physician who replaced Morell, Dr Geising, found that Hitler had been cumulatively poisoned over a period of many years by a variety of drugs in a 'truly horrifying concentration'. Geising, however, was not himself entirely blameless: in 1944 he treated Hitler's cold with a 10 per cent cocaine solution, and in his last days gave him large quantities of cocaine drops for an eye complaint.

The Dominican dictator Rafael Trujillo always signalled the imminent death of an inner-circle adviser by awarding him the Christopher Columbus medal. It became a tradition after the first recipient of the Columbus medal died from tetanus when Trujillo inadvertently stuck him with the pin.

The Malawi dictator, Dr Hastings 'one party, one leader, one government and no nonsense about it' Banda, boasted that he fed his political opponents to the crocodiles, but he was not always to be taken literally. In 1983, three of Banda's cabinet ministers and a member of the Malawi parliament died in a mysterious 'car accident'. Few at the time were convinced that the accident had been genuine. Only several years later did it emerge that the victims had had their heads staved in with tent-peg hammers.

The Equatorial Guinean leader Macias Nguema once initiated a cabinet reshuffle by clubbing his foreign minister to death.

When Saddam Hussein's war with Iran was going badly and morale was low, he called a meeting of his cabinet ministers and told them he was considering resignation. Most took the hint and insisted that he stay on. His health minister alone took him up on the offer and agreed that Saddam should step down. Saddam coolly took him into the next room, shot him in the head and sent the man's butchered remains home to his wife in a shopping bag.

In January 1971 Idi Amin went to Britain to buy a dozen Harrier jump jets, where he introduced himself to the Foreign Secretary Sir Alec Douglas-Home as 'Field Marshal Amin'. When Douglas-Home enquired what he planned to do with the aircraft, Amin told him, 'bomb Dar es Salaam'. Amin was disappointed to learn that the Harriers cost £1 million each – more than the overseas aid given annually to his near-bankrupt economy. He returned home instead with ten pairs of brown shoes and fourteen kilts costing £700; Amin's long-standing project was the creation of a personal bodyguard of 6-foot 4-inch Scotsmen, all able to play the bagpipes.

Jean-Bedel Bokassa, President of the Central African Republic, ordered the murder of one of his cabinet ministers, then served him to his colleagues for dinner. Only after the meal was over did he reveal the ingredients to his guests.

The Ethiopian dictator Colonel Mengistu Haile Miriam kept an unusual keepsake under the floorboards of his office. This was where police found the remains of his predecessor, the former Emperor Haile Selassie in 1992. According to legend, Miriam became irritated when the elderly Emperor refused to give him the numbers of his Swiss bank accounts, and had him smothered with a pillow.

In 1954 America backed Ngo Dinh Diem as the best man to keep South Vietnam from falling under the control of communism, contrary to the advice of the French, who pointed out that Diem was 'not only incapable but mad'. Diem quickly proved himself as a cruel and despotic ruler with a flair for colourful election fixes. In October 1955 the South Vietnamese were asked to choose between their former Emperor Bo Dai and Diem. When the voters arrived at the polling station they were handed two ballot papers, red for Diem and green for Bo Dai; by Vietnamese tradition, red signified good luck, green indicated bad fortune. Diem's supporters were also at hand to advise voters to put the red papers in the ballot box and to throw the green ones into the wastebasket; the few who did not take their advice were savagely beaten. In 1963 six Buddhist monks, demonstrating against Diem's corrupt rule, committed suicide in public by pouring petrol over their heads and setting fire to themselves. Unmoved, Diem offered to supply all of his country's Buddhist monks with free petrol.

In 1967, the Haitian dictator 'Papa Doc' Duvalier thwarted a coup involving nineteen Haitian army officers, led by his son-in-law Colonel Max Dominique, husband of Duvalier's daughter Marie-Denise. Afterwards, officers of the Haitian General Staff were called to Papa Doc's palace then driven to Fort Dimanche, where they found nineteen of their colleagues tied to stakes. The officers were issued with rifles and, under the gaze of Papa Doc, invited to shoot them. The public got to hear about it several days later when the president gave one of his strangest speeches yet: 'Duvalier is going to do something. He is going to take a roll-call. Major Harry Tassy, where are you? Come to your benefactor . . . absent. Lieutenant Joseph Laroche . . . absent' . . . and so on, through the nineteen names. Then, after a pause, Papa Doc cackled, 'All of them have been shot!'

The son of a cobbler, Josef Stalin worked as an apprentice in a Tbilisi shoe factory. Whenever he met cobblers later in life he surprised them by engaging them in conversations about footwear. In 1918 he commissioned a shoemaker in Tsaritsyn to make a pair to his specification; he wanted to look the part of the macho commissar. From that day on Stalin was rarely seen without his high, heavy black riding boots, even on the most inappropriate occasions and in uncomfortable conditions. In middle age, when he was plagued by corns, he simply cut holes in his favourite boots to relieve the pain. He was finally persuaded to part with them during the Second World War, when meetings with Churchill required him to make an effort and look the full part of a commander. A guest once asked Stalin why he never took his boots off even on a stiflingly hot day. The Soviet leader replied, 'So I can kick someone in the head with them so hard he'll never find all his teeth.'

According to Hitler, his greatest stroke of good fortune came thirteen years before he was born when his father, Alois Schicklgruber, changed his name to Alois Hitler. 'Heil Schicklgruber', he said, would never have caught on.

Idi Amin dispensed advice on protocol to his fellow world leaders, from President Richard Nixon to Mao Zedong. He once reminded the Israeli Prime Minister Golda Meir to pack her knickers and told Queen Elizabeth to come to Uganda 'if you want to meet a real man'. He wrote to Lord Snowdon after his split with Princess Margaret, 'Your experience will be a lesson to all of us men to be careful not to marry ladies in high positions.'

Even in the competitive field of Latin dictatorships, the Paraguayan President Francisco Solano Lopez enjoyed a reputation for ruthlessness. He had his seventy-year-old mother publicly flogged then executed when she revealed to him that he was illegitimate.

By the time Alfredo Stroessner, the son of a Bavarian brewer, seized power in 1954, Paraguay had seen off thirty-four presidents in fifty years. Stroessner immediately declared a national 'state of siege', then thoughtfully renewed it every three months for the next thirty-four years. His secret police were known locally as the *puragues* – literally, 'the hairy-footed ones' – a reminder that their raids were stealthy and brutal. Stroessner's political opponents were hurled from aeroplanes, or simply bound in wire and fed to the piranhas in the Rio Paraguay.

In the late 1960s the Chinese Communist leader Chairman Mao confessed to his aides that he secretly hoped the US would drop a nuclear bomb on a province of China and kill between ten and twenty million Chinese people. Then, said Mao, it would show the rest of the world how crazy the Americans were.

Idi Amin launched a campaign of persecution against rival tribes, handing out a mass-murder contract to his private police force, the implausibly named State Research Bureau. The SRB rounded up candidates and murdered them, then informed the victims' families that for £150 they would lead them to the body. The scheme was a huge financial success, but neighbours complained about the ceaseless din of machine-gun fire at SRB headquarters. To keep the noise down, Amin encouraged his prisoners to execute themselves by clubbing each other to death with 16-pound sledgehammers. Amin's favourite place for disposing of his victims was crocodile-infested Lake Victoria. Whenever the lights went out in Kampala, the locals knew that the hydro-electric generators on the lake's Owen Falls Dam were once again clogged with human remains.

In 1975 Jean-Bedel Bokassa announced a new regulation requiring all school girls in the Central African Republic to wear blue uniforms, fortuitously identical to those made in a factory owned by one of his seventeen wives, even though very few parents could afford to buy them. One day Bokassa's limousine was stoned by a group of about a hundred school-children protesting about the new regulations. The president had them rounded up and taken to a Bangui prison, where they were systematically beaten to death with clubs. Bokassa joined in the massacre and, according to reports, ate some of the victims.

The South Korean leader Park Chung Hee survived all but the last of several assassination attempts, including one on live TV. On 15 August 1974, the twenty-ninth anniversary of South Korean independence, Park was giving a speech at the Seoul National Theatre to an audience of visiting diplomats and members of the foreign and domestic press. A gunman emerged from the crowd and ran down the centre aisle, taking potshots at the president, who hid behind his podium, occasionally peeping out behind his Ray-Ban sunglasses. The bullets missed their target, but one fatally struck Chung's wife. Another stray felled a girl from the high school choir, who was appearing there for a singing engagement. After a brief shoot-out the assassin was overpowered by security guards. Unruffled, Park rose from his hideout, waved to the audience and, as his dying First Lady was being carried off the stage, continued his monologue. Afterwards Park and his guests heard a song performed by the choir, minus one soprano.

Idi Amin gave his Ugandan cabinet ministers a licence to kill, should any of them feel their lives were in danger from 'unruly crowds or distrusted persons', but neglected to mention that the chief executive himself was the biggest threat to their health. Any public figure who dared criticize Amin risked almost certain death; victims included the governor of the Bank of Uganda, the vice-chancellor of Makerere University, the Foreign Minister, the Chief Justice, Archbishop Luwum, plus two cabinet ministers who were beaten to death by the president himself. Amin's campaign of terror against out-of-favour colleagues often ran into logistical problems. A former government employee Francis Kalimazo was at a wedding when he learned of his own 'death' on the radio. He then realized that he was part of the backlog. The wife of an English émigré, Robert Astles, was also surprised to receive a telephone call from Amin, who offered his regret for the accidental death of her husband, and told her that she could collect the body from the city morgue. Her husband, who knew nothing of the intended assassination, was standing next to her at the time.

Macias Nguema averaged about one political killing per week in Equatorial Guinea, including ten of his original twelve cabinet members. He once amputated the fingers of his government statistician because 'he couldn't count'.

An unabashed admirer of Hitler, the Dominican dictator Rafael Trujillo equipped his secret police force with a fleet of black Volkswagen Beetles and acquired his own 'chief of Gestapo' in Colonel 'Johnny' Abbes Garcia, a talented psychopath with a predilection for the occult; Garcia claimed to be able to read his victims' auras while burning them with lighted cigarettes. Trujillo was inspired by Hitler's racial theories and wanted to 'whiten' the Dominican Republic, although he secretly wore pancake make-up to lighten his own skin, a legacy from his black grandmother. In 1937, while attending a party held in his honour, Trujillo received word that some Dominican spies in neighbouring Haiti had been discovered and killed. In a drunken rage he ordered his army to kill every Haitian resident in the Dominican Republic. In the massacre that followed, between 12,000 and 25,000 Haitians were slaughtered. Trujillo's henchmen, however, had a problem discriminating between the Haitian blacks and the dark-skinned Dominicans, who worked side by side together in the cane fields. Trujillo duly devised a test to determine if the cane-cutters were Haitian or Dominican. The Haitians spoke French Creole in which, unlike correct Spanish, the 'r' is pronounced as an 'l'. Trujillo had all the workers, at machete-point, pronounce '*perejil*' – Spanish for parsley. Those who could not correctly roll their 'r' were condemned as Haitians and butchered on the spot.

On 5 August 1972, after one of several 'visitations from God', Idi Amin gave Uganda's 50,000 Asians – mostly businessmen, doctors and nurses – ninety days to leave the country because they 'do not have the welfare of Uganda at heart'. The evacuation didn't go as smoothly as he had hoped. A few weeks later, Amin made a radio broadcast: 'Some Asians in Uganda have been painting themselves black with shoe polish. Asians are our brothers and sisters. If anyone is found painting himself with black polish, disciplinary action will be taken.'

After eliminating China's 'class enemies', Chairman Mao turned his attention to the new public enemy number one – sparrows – which, according to the Great Helmsman, were helping themselves to millions of tons of grain each year. Over a period of forty-eight hours about 80 million Chinese took to the streets and fields banging woks and gongs until the birds dropped dead of exhaustion. It was a popular move with most people; sparrows eat cereal crops and the Chinese loved fried sparrow. Teams of smiling peasants were photographed standing in front of 20-foot high mountains of dead sparrows; the most prolific sparrow-killers were awarded Mao badges, proud emblems of their revolutionary anti-sparrow zeal. Without the sparrows to control worms and other pests, however, ecological disaster followed swiftly, and 43 million Chinese starved to death.

Fickle in international relations, Idi Amin was once allied to Israel, a country that awarded him the wings of a parachute commando, which 'Big Daddy' wore with pride on his military uniform. Amin soon shifted his allegiance to Libya and Palestine, however, claiming that Israelis had deliberately poisoned the waters of the Nile, and were planning to invade Uganda and declare it a Zionist state. In 1972 he woke Jordan's King Hussein, his cabinet and military commanders in the middle of the night to tell them he had a plan to conquer Israel. His enemies were puzzled when, a year later, he was shown still sporting his coveted Israeli paratrooper wings in his likeness on Uganda's new banknotes.

To combat an infestation of beggars and layabouts in the capital of the Central African Republic, Bangui, Jean-Bedel Bokassa had them loaded on to planes and dropped into the Ubangi River.

The Paraguayan dictator Alfredo Stroessner was renowned for his extremely accurate political sense. It deserted him only once in 1948, when he found himself on the wrong side of a failed coup attempt and had to escape to the Brazilian embassy hidden in the boot of a car, an experience which earned him the nickname 'Colonel Trunk'.

Marking the anniversary of his military coup in 1977, Idi Amin invited the former British Prime Minister Edward Heath to fly to Uganda 'with his band' to play before him during the celebrations. Amin said he regretted that Mr Heath had been demoted to the obscure rank of bandleader, but noted that he understood that Heath was now one of the best bandleaders in Britain, and offered to assist the ex-PM with a supply of goats and chickens. Heath was well used to Amin's philanthropic gestures. He once started a 'Save Britain Fund', promising shiploads of vegetables to relieve economic recession, and offered to organize a whip-round of Uganda's friends, 'if you will let me know the exact position of the mess'.

The Dominican dictator Rafael Trujillo was notoriously sensitive to criticism. In 1956 a Spanish professor of literature and political science, Jesus Galindez, wrote a thesis documenting some of Trujillo's more revolting excesses, then read his dissertation to the faculty history committee at Columbia University in New York. Unfortunately for Galindez a copy of the manuscript also landed in Trujillo's lap. Twelve days later, two Dominican agents kidnapped the professor from his Manhattan apartment on Fifth Avenue and flew him to the capital of the Dominican Republic, where he was shackled by his feet, hung upside down and slowly lowered into a large pot of boiling water.

In 1978 Idi Amin planned a full-scale invasion of neighbouring Tanzania, but first decided to lull Tanzania's President Julius Nyerere into a false sense of security. He sent Nyerere a telegram: 'I want to assure you that I love you very much, and if you had been a woman I would have considered marrying you, although your head is full of grey hairs, but as you are a man, that possibility does not arise.'

'Papa Doc' Duvalier's private Haitian militia, the Tontons Macoutes, took their name from a mythical bogeyman who hunts down naughty children and kidnaps them in his bag. The Macoutes were above the law and answerable only to Papa Doc. Most were unpaid and depended on extortion for their living. A Macoute could take his or her food from the market without paying for it, take free rides in buses and taxis, and demand that neighbours bring in their harvest or hand over their belongings, land or homes. A refusal would be interpreted as an act hostile to Duvalier, and a reluctant owner could be beaten, imprisoned or killed on the spot, the victims' bodies left to lie in the street. Some Macoutes attained legendary status, thanks to their creative achievements in brutality. One such celebrated sadist was the infamous Madame Max Adolphe, who delighted in mutilating the genitals of her male prisoners. When 'Papa Doc' Duvalier died in 1971, his son Baby Doc tried to give his father's much-hated militia a makeover to make them appear more people-friendly, renaming them the 'National Security Volunteers'. The rebranding exercise never quite took off. When Baby Doc fled into exile in 1986, the public backlash against known Macoutes was fierce. Some were subjected to 'necklacing' – being set on fire by having burning petrol-soaked tyres thrown around the neck. The less fortunate were ritually eaten by their killers, their flesh having been marinated in a cheap Haitian rum called Clarin.

Stalin was famous for his gallows humour. Whenever he ran into a commissar he hadn't met for a while, he'd quip, 'Hello, haven't they shot you yet?' He also made fun of his success at getting people to confess to crimes they had never committed. 'Uncle Joe' told this joke to a man who had actually been tortured: the NKVD (the Soviet secret police agency) arrested a boy and accused him of writing *Eugene Onegin*. The boy tried to deny it. A few days later the NKVD interrogator bumped into the boy's parents. 'Congratulations,' he said. 'Your son wrote *Eugene Onegin*.' Stalin had a favourite saying at cabinet meetings: 'There is a man, there is a problem. No man, no problem.' This one-liner was guaranteed to elicit a few nervous chuckles from his confederates, most of whom also ended up being executed on their boss's orders. Stalin loved to hide behind a velvet curtain to watch the show trials of his former party colleagues and enjoyed making doodles of the enemies he planned to liquidate. In one drawing, his finance minister Nikolai Bryukhanov was depicted naked and hanging by his genitals. A caption underneath read, 'To all members of the Politburo, for all his present and future sins, Bryukhanov should be hung by his balls. If they hold up he should be considered not guilty as if in a court of law. If they give way he should be drowned in a river.' Bryukhanov was executed in 1938.

Chastisements dished out by Saddam Hussein followed a clearly defined scale of medieval barbarity. Deserters had an ear cut off. Thieves had fingers or hands cut off, depending on the source and value of stolen goods; theft of government property cost the perpetrator a hand. Liars had their backs broken; offenders were tied face-down on a wooden plank between two cement blocks and another block was dropped on the victim's spine. Informants who supplied the state police with tips that proved false had a piece of red-hot iron placed on their tongue. Homosexuals were often bound then pushed off the roof of a building. Traitors, spies, smugglers and occasionally prostitutes paid the ultimate price – beheading with a 5-foot broadsword known as al-Bashar. Saddam was inclined to kill people in public, executing underlings himself by shooting them on the spot, and sometimes giving his gun to someone else and ordering them to shoot, thus making them his accomplices. Saddam's son Uday was a chip off the old block. At a party held in honour of Suzanne Mubarak, the wife of the Egyptian president, and in full view of all the guests, Uday killed an out-of-favour aide, Kamel Hannah Jajo, by slashing him with an electric carving knife, before shooting him several times with a pistol.

Dinner guests at Idi Amin's State House were treated to some unscheduled entertainment by their host in August 1972 when, between courses, their president vanished into the kitchen and returned with the frozen head of his former commander-in-chief, Brigadier Hussein. Amin shouted abuse at the head and threw cutlery at it, then asked his guests to leave.

Long before he thought of world domination, Hitler hoped to make his fortune from a miracle baldness cure.

Born: Idi Amin Dada Oumee in 1925 (the precise date is unknown).

Died: 15 August 2003 (Amin once told a journalist he was unafraid of death because God had already told him precisely when he would die; when pressed for details, Amin said the information was 'top secret').

Also known as: Big Daddy; Dr Jaffa; the King of Scotland.

Occupation: President for Life of Uganda 1971–9 (full title 'Lord of All the Beasts of the Earth and Fishes of the Sea and Conqueror of the British Empire in Africa in General and Uganda in Particular').

Hobbies: Erecting statues to his greatest idols, Queen Victoria and Adolf Hitler; crushing the genitals of his opponents with his bare hands.

Career highlight: Carried to his inauguration as President for Life in 1975 by fourteen white Ugandans, to symbolize the 'white man's burden'.

Career lowlight: In September 1972 the *Sun* devoted its whole front page to him with just two words: 'HE'S NUTS'.

Significant others: Four wives, Sarah, Kay, Norah and Medina.

Family: An estimated forty-three children.

Style: Fetish for Scottish regalia, especially kilts and bagpipes.

Whimsical cruelty factor: 🤚🤚🤚🤚

The first dictator of the colour TV era, he ordered the decapitation of several political opponents to be transmitted live on television, specifying that the victims 'must wear white to make it easy to see the blood'.

Legacy: At least 300,000 dead; expelled his country's entire Asian population – deprived of its business class, Uganda plummeted into economic chaos.

Wit and wisdom: 'I ate them before they ate me.'

PROFILE: RAFAEL TRUJILLO

Born: Rafael Leonidas Trujillo Molina on 24 October 1891.

Died: 30 May 1961.

Also known as: Generalissimo; the Goat; El Jefe ('the Chief').

Occupation: President of the Dominican Republic 1930–61.

Hobbies: Tested the loyalty of his functionaries by demanding they let him sleep with their wives and daughters, then humiliated his underlings further by obliging them to join in.

Career highlight: Winning the 1937 Dominican Baseball League Championship with his own team, the Ciudad Trujillo Dragons.

Career lowlight: Incontinent and approaching his seventieth birthday, he was cut down in a hail of machine-gun fire on his way to visit his twenty-year-old mistress.

Significant others: Two wives, Aminta and Bienvenida.

Family: His son Ramfis survived him as head of the Armed Forces to take vengeance and empty the treasury.

Style: Ruritanian magnificence – Sergeant Pepper uniforms and dark glasses.

Whimsical cruelty factor:

Fed his enemies to the sharks; had his doctor killed after he diagnosed the Generalissimo with prostate cancer.

Legacy: Racist massacre – the deaths of up to 25,000 Haitian migrants.

Wit and wisdom: 'Cemetery is a Greek word which signifies rest for the dead and inexorable warning for the living.'

PROFILE: ALFREDO STROESSNER

Born: 3 November 1912

Also known as: The Luminous Lighthouse, Colonel Trunk.

Occupation: President of Paraguay 1954–89 (full title –
'Generalissimo Alfredo Stroessner, Legion d'Honneur,
Knight of the Order of St Michael and St George, Order
of the Condor of the Andes, Medal of the Inter-American
Junta of Defence, Collar of the Order of the Liberator and
Grand Cross of the Order of the Sun – with Diamonds').

Hobbies: Sheltering retired dictators (Pinochet, Somoza) and
an estimated 300 Nazi war criminals. An enthusiastic
human-rights abuser, he was a participant in Operation
Condor, a clandestine terrorist campaign against leftists,
and documented his torture sessions in a 5-ton archive
known as 'the Terror Files'.

Career highlight: Meeting the Duke of Edinburgh during his
tour of South America. Philip told him: 'It's a pleasant
change to be in a country that isn't ruled by its people.'

Career lowlight: While visiting his favourite mistress for their
regular Thursday afternoon siesta, he heard that he had
been ousted by his protégé and second-in-command,
General Andres Rodriguez.

Significant others: Wife Dona and various teenage mistresses,
including a fifteen-year-old he became involved with well

into his seventies. Sons Gustavo and Freddie Jnr, plus numerous illegitimate children.

Style: Military chic. Despite wearing enough gold braid to hang an opposition party, according to the novelist Graham Greene, Stroessner looked like 'the amiable well-fed host of a Bavarian *bierstube*'.

Whimsical cruelty factor: 🗡️ 🗡️ 🗡️ 🗡️

His imaginative torturer-in-chief Pastor Coronel conducted interrogations with interviewees who were immersed in the *pileta* – a bathtub full of human excrement.

Legacy: Second only to North Korea's Kim Il Sung as the world's most durable despot; tortured or killed an estimated 200,000 people during his thirty-five-year rule.

CHAPTER 2
Paranoiacs

The first of a long line of Paraguayan dictators, Dr Jose Gaspar Rodriguez de Francia was constantly haunted by the fear of treachery and assassination, and created a vast network of spies. *El Supremo*, as he was known, passed a law requiring men to wear hats so that everyone could tip them to him as he went by, but in time he became so fearful for his personal safety that whenever he went out no one else was allowed on the streets, and the doors and windows of houses had to be shuttered. Anyone caught out on the street when he passed had to prostrate themselves or risk being put to the sword by his escort of armed cavalry. He had every tree and shrub in the capital Asunción removed in case they were concealing assassins. Eventually Francia became a total recluse, hiding in his palace attended by just four servants, employing his sister to unroll his cigars to check if they had been tampered with, communicating with the outside world only through his barber. Every year Francia sent about 400 political enemies to his Chamber of Truth, where, in between interrogations, inmates were chained to dungeon walls and denied medical care or the use of sanitary facilities. He jailed so many people, it was said, that Paraguay's blacksmiths couldn't keep up with the demand for shackles. Francia personally supervised firing squads, but hated to waste bullets. If a prisoner wasn't killed at the first attempt, he had them run through with bayonets.

In 1927 Josef Stalin became depressed and called upon the famous Russian neurologist and psychiatrist Vladimir Bekhterev. The physician diagnosed 'grave paranoia' and advised Stalin's immediate retirement. It was the last advice Bekhterev ever gave; arrangements for his funeral were made soon afterwards.

Amid rumours of madness and mania, the Burmese dictator General Ne Win made regular trips to a Viennese psychiatrist. Ne Win's rule was defined by bizarre whims, omens and astrological predictions. The general awoke one morning and announced that it had been revealed to him in a dream that the Burmese should stop driving on the left-hand side of the road and switch to the right. As most of the cars in Rangoon were old, British, right-hand-drive models, Burma quickly became a world leader in road fatalities. Ne Win was obsessed with numerology, especially his lucky number nine. He staged major events on dates containing the number nine – 9 September became a national holiday. He made his pilots circle nine times before landing his plane, and tore down his old palace and built a new one with 9-foot-high ceilings and every measurement rounded to the nearest nine. In 1987, after consulting his astrologer, Ne Win withdrew Burma's decimal currency from circulation, introducing banknotes in 45 and 90 kyat denominations, both divisible by the mystically desirable number nine, causing economic havoc and widespread financial ruin. There were ninety-nine Buddhist monks at hand for Ne Win's last public appearance in 1988, just before he stepped down.

Nicolae Ceausescu operated the world's most pervasive surveillance system. Every Romanian telephone manufactured during his dictatorship was issued with a bugging device as standard.

The Paraguayan dictator Francisco Solano Lopez, who was short, fat and bandy-legged, had a penchant for extravagant military uniforms to help disguise his physical shortcomings. Lopez acquired a classic Napoleonic fixation after being told, during a trip to France in 1853, that he bore a strong resemblance to the late, great Corsican. He returned home with seventy-three pairs of patent leather boots made by Napoleon III's personal shoemaker, and a girlfriend, Eliza Lynch, an Irish courtesan he had found in Paris. Lopez immediately redesigned Paraguay's military uniforms to look identical to those worn by the French, and ordered for himself an exact replica of Napoleon Bonaparte's crown. He also took to wearing one hand tucked inside his jacket at all times. In the grip of Napoleonic delusion, Lopez spent most of his eight-year reign waging a hopeless war on three fronts against his neighbouring enemies, Argentina, Brazil and Uruguay. Outnumbered by their combined armies by ten to one, Lopez made up the numbers by drafting boys and old men. At one point he attempted to rout the Brazilian army by sending out a battalion of twelve-year-olds wearing false beards. Any show of dissent against Lopez's increasingly desperate military orders brought imprisonment, torture and lingering death. He trained his troops so hard and for so long that many didn't even live long enough to see a battle. As Paraguay's demoralized, ill-equipped and mostly starving soldiers awaited death, Lopez's mistress 'Madame' Lynch tried to raise morale by touring the army camps in a black coach, followed by several carriage-loads of her extensive wardrobe of Parisian gowns and a grand piano. Lopez meanwhile always fled the battlefield at the slightest suspicion of danger, and when he ran, his entourage were always obliged to flee with him; to have shown less fear than the commander-in-chief was considered worse than treason. As the military position grew ever more hopeless, Lopez organized a spying system which encouraged every third man in his army to spy on his comrades and to shoot anyone, including officers, who showed any sign of cowardice. Many took the opportunity of shooting their officers first to avoid being shot themselves. Widespread paranoia among the ranks led to many of his men marching into battle backwards, because they feared their own side more than the enemy. When Lopez's most senior commander found himself surrounded and facing certain defeat, he opted to blow his own brains out rather than face his president, but he missed, shooting only one eye out. Convinced of a vast conspiracy to overthrow him, Lopez ordered hundreds of random executions, including those of two of his brothers and two brothers-in-law, scores of top government and military officials, and several foreign diplomats; he had his victims killed by lance thrusts to save on ammunition. Suspicious of yet another intrigue against him, this time by Paraguay's aristocracy, he solved the problem by putting all of the sons of his country's ruling class into a single regiment, then sent them on a suicidal attack, unarmed and barefoot; all but two died. In the end Lopez's military incompetence, combined with a refusal to allow any of his men to surrender, reduced the male population of Paraguay by 90 per cent. Feeling depressed, the president organized a mass suicide pact, ordering what was left of the entire population of his nation's capital to follow him into the jungle, but then he changed his mind at the last minute. In 1870 Brazilian soldiers caught the obese and grossly-overdecorated Lopez, and ended his Napoleonic career with a bullet. Eliza Lynch, the mistress who had borne him five children, escaped with most of Paraguay's treasury for comfortable exile in Paris.

Mussolini was very superstitious. He never dined at a table of thirteen people, and liked to ward off the 'evil eye' by touching his testicles. He was also obsessed with hygiene, and adopted the Roman-style straight-arm greeting as the fascist salute because he hated shaking hands with people.

The rarely used salutation Royal Dictator was first applied in 1938 to the paranoid King Carol II of Romania, a cousin of Queen Elizabeth II. King Carol had some of the most architecturally important buildings in Bucharest demolished so that the sights of his machine-guns could get a clear line of fire at the approaches to his palace.

In 1924 Albania found a new political leader in the person of Ahmed Zogu, a chieftain of the Gheg clan in the Mati valley.

Zogu happily began his reign as president, until he was shot and wounded in Parliament, and a revolution drove him into exile. Six months later, Zogu returned and staged a coup, and on 1 December 1928 he accepted the 'illustrious crown of the historic Albanian throne' and declared himself King Zog I, at last giving himself an excuse for indulging his weakness for spectacular Ruritanian uniforms. For his coronation he ordered an outfit comprising rose-coloured breeches, gold spurs and a gold crown weighing over 7½ pounds. The occasion was marked by six days of public holidays, and planeloads of confetti were dropped over the capital Tirana. Government officials stencilled 'Long live the King' on the walls of public buildings, and shopkeepers were threatened with fines unless they displayed Zogu's portrait in their window. In some parts a huge letter 'Z' was burnt on to the hillside. In spite of these forced displays of enthusiasm, King Zog was anything but popular. His struggle to become political master of Albania had been achieved on the back of murder, torture, blackmail and bribery on a scale never before seen in the history of his country. By 1928 he was involved in as many as 600 *giakmarrje* (blood feuds), with various people he had upset during his leadership, including at least half a dozen Albanian warrior chieftains and numerous politicians. It made him the subject of an estimated fifty-five assassination attempts. Self-incarceration was the best defence. Except on national holidays, Zogu hardly ever appeared in public. As he was well over 6 feet tall with red hair, he made a conspicuous target in a country where most men were dark and under 5 foot 6. On the very rare occasions he ventured outside, his mother acted as chaperone – according to the strict rules of the Albanian blood feud, no man can be harmed if accompanied in public by a woman. Zogu spent most of his reign as a recluse in his capital city, Tirana, playing poker and chain-smoking up to 150 cigarettes a day. His nerves were so frayed that on his wedding day he banned photographers' flashbulbs, and not once during the ten days' commanded public rejoicing did he or his bride, the Hungarian Countess Geraldine Apponyi, dare to appear at the palace window to acknowledge their subjects. Zogu presided over a huge royal family, including six sisters, a half-brother, several nieces and nephews, a queen mother who patrolled the royal kitchen to protect him from food poisoning, and an elderly 'godfather', known as 'the scabby one', who carried revolvers in the pockets of his morning suit. Zogu rarely left his country for fear of revolt in his absence, but in February 1931, aged thirty-four, he collapsed with severe chest pains and was obliged to consult a specialist in Vienna. The visit, the first time Zogu had left Albania since 1924, was conducted in such secrecy that even some of his most senior ministers were unaware that he was missing. The trip resulted in the most famous of his many assassination attempts. On 21 February, as Zogu was leaving a performance of *Pagliacci* at the Vienna Opera House, two gunmen opened fire at him as he was climbing into the car. The bullets meant for him were stopped by his ADC Topallaj and his minister Libohava. The trial of his two Albanian assailants, Noloc Gjeloshi and Aziz Cemi, was held at Ried in Austria. Although a police investigation found evidence that the would-be assassins were in the pay of the Yugoslavian government, the men claimed they had acted alone, on impulse. Gjeloshi explained, 'When an Albanian has not got himself in hand, he has a revolver in it.'

The Romanian dictator Nicolae Ceausescu and his wife Elena shared a phobia of germs. The presidential couple went on numerous publicity walkabouts, photo opportunities that required them to shake a few hands and kiss small children, but they were terrified that they would catch a terminal disease from contact with the Romanian masses. The problem was solved to their satisfaction by their secret police, the Securitate, who rounded up a few volunteers weeks in advance and had them locked up and regularly disinfected in readiness for the big day.

The Albanian dictator Enver Hoxha lived in fear of joint invasion by 'Anglo-American Imperialists' and 'Russo-Bulgar revisionists'. In 1950 Hoxha ordered the construction of a prototype concrete bunker, complete with a sniper's gun slit with 360° visibility. When the small, mushroom-shaped edifice was complete he asked the chief engineer if he was confident that it could withstand a full assault from a tank. He replied in the affirmative. Hoxha then insisted that the engineer stand inside his creation while it was bombarded by a tank. After about fifteen minutes the shell-shocked engineer emerged, shaken and deafened, but unscathed. Hoxha was impressed, and immediately ordered mass construction of the bunkers. From 1950 until his death in 1985 he built around 800,000 of them, one for every four Albanians, covering the entire countryside and costing from one-third to one-half of his nation's pitifully small resources. No one invaded.

After receiving an anonymous death threat through the post, Nicolae Ceausescu ordered his secret police to secure handwriting samples from the entire Romanian population.

On a visit to China in 1965, the British Second World War hero Viscount Montgomery asked Chairman Mao, 'If you died today, who would take over?' Mao named Liu Shaoqi, then head of state. Montgomery recounted this anecdote to the world's press, which revealed that Liu Shaoqi was the Number Two man in China, and in doing so he inadvertently signed Liu's death warrant. The newspaper headlines convinced the paranoid Mao that Liu was scheming to take over. In response, Mao unleashed the Cultural Revolution and jettisoned his former comrade. Liu, now pilloried as the 'Number One capitalist roader', died in prison deprived of food and medical attention.

In June 1978 Nicolae Ceausescu and his wife Elena arrived on a full state visit to Britain, their reward for placing a large order for British aerospace technology. It was a spectacular event, the presidential couple met by a gun salute, a drive with the Queen in the royal landau and accommodation at Buckingham Palace. The Queen was baffled by the discovery that her guests had brought with them their own bedlinen and a host of minders including a personal food-taster. She was also alarmed by Nicolae's habit of washing his hands every time he shook hands with anyone, a trick he repeated after shaking hands with the Queen herself. One morning during the Ceausescus' three-day visit, Nicolae was spotted at 6 a.m. walking in the palace gardens with his minders. He had naturally assumed that his host had bugged his room, as *he* would certainly have done, so the garden was the safest place for him to talk. The rest of the visit and the aerospace deal went off without a hitch, until it was time to pay up. Romania was so strapped for cash that, when pressed for the money, Ceausescu offered part payment in ice cream, yogurt and strawberries.

Security around the North Korean dictator Kim Il Sung was so tight on trips abroad that his aides carried a special toilet with built-in monitoring equipment to keep tabs on his health. It also served another private function, which was to keep the Great Leader's deposits away from the clutches of foreign intelligence agencies; both the American and Soviet secret services were in the habit of placing 'traps' in the plumbing of buildings frequented by world leaders.

The Haitian government radio station, Radio Commerce, occasionally interrupted its regular programme to broadcast for hours the popular song '*Di fe den kaill la*' ('Fire in the house') – the anthem traditionally played whenever there was an attempt to overthrow their president. Papa Doc survived nine attempts to be deposed. The first came in 1958 when a gang of eight rebels, including three ex-deputy sheriffs from Miami, Florida and New York, 'invaded' Haiti and advanced on the presidential palace at Port-au-Prince in a stolen jeep. On their way to the capital the jeep broke down. Posing as tourists, the invading army flagged down a taxi-bus and hijacked it. As revolution by taxi was not expected, they were able to drive into the Dessalines barracks unopposed, and disarm the handful of sleeping soldiers before the Haitian military were even aware of their presence. The weapons they had expected to find stored at the barracks, however, had been moved to the palace basement. Papa Doc, who had no idea that only eight men were involved in the invasion, packed his bags and made ready to flee to a foreign embassy. The rebels showed their hand though, by sending one of their hostages out to buy them a packet of cigarettes; he was captured and the true scale of the invading army was revealed to the embarrassed authorities. Duvalier ordered his troops to storm the barracks and all eight men were executed on the spot.

The Comoros Islands dictator Ali Soilih was highly superstitious. Tipped off by a witch doctor that he would be killed by a white man with a black dog, he had every black dog on the island put down.

Enver Hoxha was thought to have had a double, an Albanian village dentist who was abducted by the secret police, the Sigurimi, and surgically enhanced to make him appear to be the president's identical twin. Hoxha's plan was to keep his lookalike close at hand in case of an invasion, when he would be sacrificed to enemy soldiers while the president escaped to the mountains. The double spent ten years in relative luxury in a compound within the presidential palace, and was brought out to stand in for his president at official events every now and then. When Hoxha died and the communists were overthrown, the double was attacked by a mob who thought he was the ghost of the former dictator.

Stalin held all-night drinking parties, where he would deliberately make all the members of his inner circle drunk to loosen their tongues while he quietly sipped a glass of Georgian red. Visitors to his dacha would be asked to guess the temperature outside and then have to drink as many glasses of vodka as the number of degrees by which they were wrong.

His functionaries, never sure whether their evening out was going to end with a firing squad, found the drinking sessions such an ordeal that they secretly bribed the waiters to bring them coloured water instead of alcohol. Due in part to Stalin's notorious drinking binges, several top Politburo members became alcoholics.

The British Liberal Party leader David Steel once gave Nicolae Ceausescu a black Labrador puppy called Gladstone, which the Romanian leader renamed Corbu (Raven). Despite his amicable relationship with foreign powers, Ceausescu only ever employed ambassadors who were not fluent in foreign languages – because he was afraid they might defect. Thus, the most important job for the Romanian ambassador in London was his weekly trip to Sainsbury's to purchase Winalot and dog biscuits for Corbu, before sending them on to Romania in the diplomatic bag. Incidentally, 'Comrade Corbu' became the subject of much popular myth; Ceausescu was said to be so fond of his dog that he gave it its own house, telephone and motorcade, and promoted it to the rank of Colonel in the Romanian army.

To ensure the conservation of supplies of his favourite dish, Enver Hoxha made it illegal to fish for red-speckled trout; the penalty for catching one was fifteen years' hard labour.

Nicolae Ceausescu banned long hair on males, denim, short skirts and Romania's three favourite TV programmes, all of them British imports; *The Avengers*, *The Forsyte Saga* and *The Saint*.

Enver Hoxha banned beards and long hair, even on visiting foreigners. Albanian-border barbers were employed to snip excess hair from all foreigners entering the country; the degree of hairiness was then noted in police files.

In 1966 Doctor Hastings Banda became the first president of the newly-established republic of Malawi. Dr Banda, an Anglophile with a taste for Homburg hats, strove hard to keep modernity beyond his borders. He wasted almost all of his country's education budget on a bizarre 'Eton in the jungle', offering cricket, cold showers and classical education in Latin and Greek. He employed airport barbers to clip long-haired males on arrival, and demanded that short-skirted female visitors open their suitcases and change into something that covered their knees. Banda also imposed the local Chichewa as the new official national language. He had forgotten, however, that he did not speak a word of Chichewa himself, and throughout his entire thirty-year presidency had to communicate through an interpreter.

Nicolae Ceausescu was one of several dictators who tried to achieve economic growth by increasing his country's population. In an attempt to double Romania's populace in a generation, he imposed a 'celibacy tax' on women of childbearing age who failed to give birth to at least four children, although his own wife Elena had only three. Every month Romanian women were forced to undergo body searches in the presence of government agents, known as the 'menstrual police', to ensure that they weren't secretly using contraceptive devices. Expectant mothers who failed to produce a baby on the due date were arrested for questioning. Women who did not bear children, including those who were incapable, were obliged to pay up to 10 per cent of their monthly salaries. Sex education was also banned; books about human reproduction were classified as 'state secrets' to be read only by doctors. The Burmese dictator General Ne Win also outlawed all forms of birth control to make sure that Burma's population kept pace with that of its two great neighbouring countries, India and China. It was a formidable assignment for Burmese mothers, given that they were outnumbered by their neighbours by nearly forty-seven to one.

Enver Hoxha banned private ownership of consumer items that his country couldn't provide, that no Albanian could ever afford and that few had even seen, including television sets and private cars. No one was allowed to drive a car without a permit and only two permits were ever issued outside of the Albanian Communist Party. In 1992, when Albania was opened to foreigners, there were only 150 cars in the entire country. However there were few complaints about the lack of consumer goods: the penalty for being heard saying that the shops weren't full was fifteen years' hard labour.

The South Korean dictator Park Chung Hee hated lefty students, and declared an Anti-Long Hair Campaign which authorized his police to seize hirsute Koreans in the street and shave them right there on the spot. He was even tougher on communists, as Article 10 of his country's constitution offered prize money to anyone who killed one or caused a communist to commit suicide.

Nicolae Ceausescu's father Andrutsa, a notorious drunk, was with some friends in a pub in the centre of Bucharest when his son appeared on television making a speech. Ceausescu senior told his fellow drinkers not to take any notice of anything his son said, quipping, 'He tells nothing but lies'. The next day the pub had vanished to make way for a cheese shop.

Born: Nicolae Andrutu Ceausescu on 26 January 1918.

Died: 25 December 1989.

Also known as: Comrade Supreme Commander; Genius of the Carpathians; The Conducator; Nasty Nick.

Occupation: President of Romania 1965–89.

Hobbies: Kitsch monumental building works; bear hunting with his Holland and Holland custom British rifle.

Career highlights: Suppressed free speech and travel by introducing the world's first typewriter licence, banning maps and making it illegal to talk to foreigners.

Career lowlight: Execution by firing squad on live TV on Christmas Day.

Significant others: Wife Elena, 'world-renowned chemist and scientist'.

Family: Twenty-seven close relatives, all holding top party and state positions, including daughter Zoia and playboy son Nicu, who once escaped prosecution after running over a girl while drunk.

Style: A fussy dresser – convinced that foreign agents were trying to poison his clothes, he had the state police make all of his clothes for him, including his favourite German-style hunting outfits, under surveillance in a specially constructed warehouse; each garment was worn once then burned.

Whimsical cruelty factor:

Hundreds of villages were slated for 'renovation', Ceausescu's euphemism for ethnic cleansing; he once destroyed a dam and let it flood a nearby village full of Hungarians.

Legacy: 'Death camp' orphanages; widespread famine caused by catastrophic 'agricultural reforms'.

Wit and wisdom: 'And they call that genocide?' – Elena Ceausescu at their trial, when the state prosecutor pointed out that thirty-four people had died in rioting.

PROFILE: ENVER HOXHA

Born: 16 October 1908.

Died: 11 April 1985.

Also known as: Great Teacher; the Ugly One.

Occupation: President of the People's Socialist Republic of Albania 1945–85 (full title 'Comrade Chairman Prime Minister, Foreign Minister, Minister of War, Commander-in-Chief of the People's Army'; later he added the word 'Supreme' in front of 'Comrade', and adopted the mysterious epithet 'Sole Force').

Hobbies: A committed atheist, he had priests buried alive.

Career highlights: Banned beards, Western pop music, Greek Christian names for babies, kissing on television and foreign travel. Albanians caught trying to leave their country, mostly by swimming the three-mile channel to Corfu, were shot and their bodies strung up on public display.

Career lowlight: As a communist guerrilla fighter, he was forced to subsist on boiled gravel for three years.

Significant others: Wife Nexhmije.

Style: More Stalinist than Stalin.

Whimsical cruelty factor: 🥊 🥊 🥊

He dismissed a prime minister by shooting him dead at dinner.

Legacy: 800,000 concrete bunkers; tidy streets (dropping refuse was punishable by a spell in a labour camp).

Wit and wisdom: 'Albania and China are very important countries. Together they make up 25 per cent of the world's population.' – on a visit to the People's Republic of China.

Born: Shu Maung on 24 May 1911.

Died: 5 December 2002.

Also known as: The Old Man; The Puppet Master; Number One.

Occupation: President of Burma 1962–88.

Hobbies: An obsession with the number nine; drinking, gambling and women – said to have bathed daily in dolphins' blood to regain his youthful vigour.

Career highlight: In 1962 he seized power from prime minister U Nu, beginning four decades of military rule.

Career lowlight: Kicked out of university in 1931 after failing his biology exam, he decided to start a revolution; his first act in power in 1962 was to massacre protesting students and to blow up the students' union building.

Significant others: Married five times, twice to a history professor and once to an Italian actress.

Style: Increasingly obtuse behaviour; he imagined himself to be the reincarnation of an ancient Burmese warrior king and liked to dress up as one.

Whimsical cruelty factor: 🥊 🥊 🥊

Beat a colleague to death with a club on a golf course.

Legacy: Economic disaster, largely thanks to his numerical obsession with the number nine; the machinery of a ruthless authoritarian state.

Wit and wisdom: 'Damn fools. Motherf**kers. Why do you want a press conference? What do you want me to say?'– at his one and only press conference.

CHAPTER 3
Kleptocrats

Peruvian President Alberto Fujimori worked hand in hand with his mysterious associate Vladimiro Montesinos – a sleazy lawyer who had once sold Peruvian army secrets to the CIA, and in 1990 assisted Fujimori's election bid by arranging to have all legal records of his history of tax evasion conveniently disappear. Fujimori's sister ran a charity, collecting used clothes from Japan and distributing them to the poor of Peru. The clothes were stored in the basement of the presidential palace, where the Fujimori family could pick through them, keeping the best for themselves. One Christmas the president told an army colonel that he had a present for him. He escorted the lucky colonel to the basement and invited him to pick what he wanted. When Fujimori's estranged wife blew the whistle on the great second-hand clothes scam, the president had her locked up in the palace. Later, after the First Couple divorced, she announced that she was running for president against him. He responded by passing a new law prohibiting a sitting president's relatives from running for high office. Montesinos's reward, meanwhile, was his appointment as Head of the Peruvian police force. In that role, Montesinos bribed judges and politicians to support Fujimori's increasingly dictatorial rule, and videotaped them taking the bribes. This ploy worked well for several years, until the videos were leaked to a Peruvian TV journalist, who sensationally played them live on air. The bribery scandal sent both Fujimori and Montesinos into exile. Montesinos fled to Venezuela, where he underwent extensive plastic surgery and disappeared again, his whereabouts and new facial features unknown. Fujimori, meanwhile, escaped to Brunei and then Japan, where he became the first dictator in history to resign his office by e-mail.

In 1939, invasion by Benito Mussolini forced Albania's heavily braided despot Ahmed Zogu – 'King Zog I' – and his wife to flee into exile, accompanied by their huge family and a couple of thousand officials. The Zogus sat out the war years at the Ritz Hotel in London, where they thought it wise to sell their bright red Mercedes, a wedding present from Adolf Hitler and inconveniently identical to the one used by the Führer himself. Unfortunately, the cheque for £800, which they received in exchange for the car, bounced and the police were called in. The car was located in Scotland, but had been sold on a couple of times and Zogu had to buy it back. Zogu found himself in the news again when he lost his wallet to a pickpocket in Harrods. By an amazing stroke of good fortune, the wallet was recovered containing £1,000 in cash. The story attracted widespread attention in the press and seemed to confirm suspicions that Zogu had escaped from Albania with the entire national treasury. Later, Zogu tried to buy *The Times*, but when he discovered it was not for sale he settled for the less influential *Kensington and Chelsea Post* instead.

While Haiti became the poorest country in the western hemisphere, President 'Papa Doc' Duvalier raised corruption to an art form, diverting millions of dollars in foreign-aid money into his own bank account. A favourite fundraising scheme was the handing out of medals of honour to foreign leaders in exchange for small 'loans'. The Cuban strongman Fulgencio Batista was awarded Haiti's highest, and newly invented, medal in exchange for $4 million. Papa Doc also hit upon a way of literally bleeding his own people dry. His militia, the Tontons Macoutes, had a daily round-up of thousands of Haitians and marched them to the nearest blood bank, where each was given £1 – about a week's wages – in exchange for a litre of blood. The blood was then sent on to the United States, where it was sold for transfusion at £12 a litre. Papa Doc dreamed of building a new Haitian city, a permanent memorial to his megalomania – Duvalierville. A variety of novel methods were employed to raise money for the project. Local businessmen were 'invited' to contribute: but those who declined had their premises burned down and looted. Other reluctant donors were imprisoned, tortured and killed. Another successful fundraiser was the use of roadblocks to collect impromptu tolls. Telephone subscribers were surprised to find that they too had been charged an extra levy to fund the building project, especially as Haiti's telephones had not worked for twenty years. Unlike the fundraising projects, Duvalierville was not a success and was never finished . . . because most of the money went directly into Papa Doc's bank account.

President Joseph Mobutu of Zaire was ranked the seventh richest man in the world when his country was among the poorest – a man so rich, it was said, he could write a personal cheque to pay off his country's entire foreign debt. Mobutu's conspicuous consumption was unparalleled. He chartered a French Concorde to fly his family to Europe on monthly shopping trips, had pink champagne flown in from Paris, mussels flown in from Belgium and prostitutes delivered from Scandinavia. In order to build himself a model farm in the Zaire jungle, he sent a government jet to Venezuela thirty-two times to bring back 5,000 long-haired sheep.

When Papa Doc discovered that tourism in his country was down by 70 per cent, he was torn between his need for revenue and his natural mistrust of foreign troublemakers. He hit upon a compromise. After launching a publicity drive to tempt the visitors back, he had the corpse of a dissident flown into the capital Port-au-Prince, where it was left to rot in public. It was strategically placed by an exit from the airport, next to a sign which read 'Welcome to Haiti'.

The corrupt and light-fingered nature of the Philippines' dictator Ferdinand Marcos is legendary. As well as appropriating up to a third of all loans to the Philippines in the form of kickbacks and commissions, Marcos also oversaw foreign investment in his country – for a small fee. A *New York Times* report found that a US nuclear power company had paid him tens of millions of dollars in bribes to allow them to build on Philippine land. As it turned out, it was money not well spent: the power station was never used, having been built over an earthquake zone, and thus in no way viable.

Nicolae Ceausescu tried to pay off huge foreign debts by exporting almost all of his country's agricultural production, resulting in food rationing and near famine. Scornful of reports that his people didn't have enough to eat, he complained that Romanians ate too much, and he introduced the revolutionary Ceausescu Diet, a 'scientific' regimen mysteriously free of the protein-rich staples Romanians missed most, especially meat and dairy products. To show that production targets were actually being met, he staged visits to the countryside where he was filmed inspecting displays of meat and fruit. The film crews alone knew that the food was mostly made from wood and polystyrene.

While his country was officially rated one of the poorest in the world, Jean-Bedel Bokassa, ruler of the former French colony Central African Republic, spent £10 million on a forty-eight-hour coronation binge to celebrate his promotion from president to emperor in 1977, a bill footed by France under the heading 'humanitarian aid'. The coronation ceremony, designed by world-famous French decorator Jean-Pierre Dupont, required the purchase of 100 limousines and 130 thoroughbred horses. The guests drank 65,000 bottles of champagne served by an army of waiters imported from Paris, and were entertained by a 120-piece orchestra. The Paris-based jeweller Claude Bertrand was commissioned to make Bokassa's crown, which was heavily encrusted with diamonds including a massive 58-carat showpiece, while Bokassa sat on a 2-ton solid gold throne made in the form of an eagle sitting upright with wings outstretched, wearing two leopard-skin mantles. Although all of the world's top political leaders were asked to attend the ceremony, most, including Britain and the US, returned their invitations. However, several foreign dignitaries, including ambassadors from Italy and West Germany, did turn up to the imperial banquet held in the capital, Bangui. They were unaware that Bokassa had arranged to have twelve selected inmates from the local prison butchered and served to his dinner guests as 'roast beef'.

'Papa Doc' Duvalier, who pocketed around $15 million a year in US aid, once kept the American ambassador Benson Timmons waiting for five weeks for an audience, then gave him a lecture on how an ambassador should behave. Papa Doc's rule of terror and widespread theft was also punctuated by unpredictable, random acts of benevolence. In 1973 a group of trade unionists who had been imprisoned for two years for daring to strike for higher pay were unexpectedly released and invited to Papa Doc's palace. To their astonishment, each was pardoned and handed an envelope containing a large amount of cash.

After her husband's death in exile, Imelda Marcos made a triumphant return to the Philippines, corruption charges notwithstanding. When asked if she had any intention of returning the suspected £6 billion stolen from the national treasury, she responded in the negative: 'If you give it back, it means you've stolen it.' She went on to justify her notorious extravagance by revealing a hitherto unknown medical condition: 'I'm allergic to ugliness.'

In the 1980s a Western Christian group, the World Reformed Alliance, sent 20,000 free Bibles to Romania where Nicolae Ceausescu had promised to distribute them. When the Bibles arrived Ceausescu confiscated the lot and had them pulped to ease a national toilet-paper shortage. The quality of Romanian pulping was so poor, however, that words such as 'God' and 'Jeremiah' were still clearly visible on the rolls of recycled toilet paper.

In January 1971 the dying 'Papa Doc' Duvalier showed off his parenting skills by introducing to the world his successor, his nineteen-year-old son Jean-Claude, once described by a French journalist as 'a prematurely overweight sports-car enthusiast', and hitherto known by his schoolmates as 'Tete-Panier' ('Basket-Head'). Papa Doc explained, 'We all know that Caesar Augustus was nineteen when he took into his hands Rome's destinies and that his reign remains "the century of Augustus".' As Papa Doc spoke mostly in French to his Haitian people, 90 per cent of them couldn't understand him; those who could follow assumed it was a joke. Three months later the ailing Papa Doc died and 'Baby Doc' became the youngest president in the world. True to family tradition, in his first test at the polls Baby Doc was re-elected with 99 per cent of the vote. In 1981 the IMF gave $22 million to the treasury of Haiti, only to discover two days later that $20 million of this had been withdrawn by Baby Doc, partly to appease his fantastically overindulgent wife Michele. She spent $50,000 a month to fly flowers from Miami to Haiti and used to crank up the air conditioning so she could wear her fur coats indoors.

PROFILE: FRANÇOIS DUVALIER

Born: 14 April 1907.

Died: 21 April 1971.

Also known as: 'Papa Doc'.

Occupation: President of Haiti 1957–71 (full title 'Lord and Master of this Land of Haiti').

Hobbies: Voodoo – when he needed advice on matters of state, he claimed he got it by sitting in his bathtub wearing a black top hat while consulting the entrails of a dead goat.

Career highlights: Keeping domestic dissent low and foreign bank accounts high.

Career lowlight: Spending two years in hiding from the government of the day – dressed as a woman.

Significant others: Wife Simone, 'Mama Doc'.

Family: Son and heir Jean-Claude, 'Baby Doc'.

Style: Black suits and bulging holsters; kept visiting Western journalists on their toes by fingering his desk 'paperweight' (a .45 revolver) and a .357 Magnum he kept under his cushion.

Whimsical cruelty factor: 🥊🥊🥊

His private militia, the Tontons Macoutes, nailed prisoners' scrotums to a wall then unshackled the victims, daring them to escape.

Legacy: Sixty thousand political enemies killed and countless more tortured by the Tontons Macoutes death squads; destruction of Haiti's economy.

Wit and wisdom: 'I am not a dictator. I am humble country doctor.'

Born: 22 February 1921.

Died: 3 November 1996.

Also known as: Papa Bok; the Ogre of Berengo.

Occupation: President of the Central African Republic 1966–79.

Hobbies: Eating the opposition.

Career highlights: Spent £10 million, more than his country's annual budget, on a forty-eight-hour coronation binge to celebrate his promotion to 'emperor'; also claimed that he was the thirteenth apostle of the Catholic Church, secretly appointed by the Pope.

Career lowlight: Fled the country in 1979, but forgot to dispose of the contents of his fridge, which included the whole frozen body of a schoolteacher hanging on a freezer hook.

Significant others: Seventeen wives.

Family: Loved children – had fifty-three of his own – but couldn't eat a whole one.

Style: Napoleonic fixation.

Whimsical cruelty factor: 👍 👍 👍 👍

He once made a point at a public press conference by hammering a journalist into submission with the weighted end of his swagger stick; served up political opponents to visiting dignitaries as 'roast beef'.

Legacy: Two thousand dead and at least $120 million missing from the national treasury.

Wit and wisdom: 'My grandfather was a very keen cannibal, you know.' – to US Ambassador William Dale.

Born: Joseph-Désiré Mobutu on 14 October 1930.

Died: 7 September 1997.

Also known as: The Big Man; The Leopard; The Messiah.

Occupation: President of Zaire 1965–97 (regularly changed his official title from the Marshal to the Supreme Emperor to King of Zaire).

Hobbies: Shopping – his garden had a runway big enough to accommodate the Air France Concorde he regularly used to buy his groceries from Paris and Brussels.

Career highlight: Theft of about $4 billion in foreign aid.

Career lowlight: Overthrown and exiled in May 1997.

Significant others: First wife Marie-Antoinette, second wife Bobi and his mistress, Bobi's identical twin.

Style: Sharkskin suits, leopard-skin pillbox hats and Buddy Holly sunglasses – the best dressed dictator since Mussolini.

Whimsical cruelty factor: 🐾 🐾 🐾

Organized nightly helicopter flights to dump the bodies of his political opponents into the river Congo.

Legacy: The doctrine of self-help, referred to as Article 15 of the constitution – i.e. everyone from the smallest official to the highest government office helped themselves; meanwhile the national economy shrank to the level it had been in 1958.

CHAPTER 4
Megalomaniacs

After leading a revolt against French rule in 1807, a black former slave Henry Christophe became president of the newly-created Republic of Haiti. He was obsessed with European royalty and wanted to create a replica court of his own, including an entire new aristocracy of Haitian princes, dukes, counts, barons and knights, based exactly on the British model. In 1811, dressed as his favourite monarch King George III, Henry had himself crowned the first King of Haiti, Sovereign of Tortuga, Gonave and other adjacent Islands, Destroyer of Tyranny, Regenerator and Benefactor of the Haitian Nation, Creator of her Moral, Political and Martial Institutions, First Crowned Monarch of the New World, Defender of the Faith, Founder of the Royal and Military Order of Saint-Henry. During his coronation he insisted upon drawing attention to his country's chief export by having himself anointed with chocolate syrup. The new Haitian president-king was a fanatical builder of palaces and monuments. He built a massive new fortress, Citadel Henry, at the summit of a high mountain peak, fortified by batteries holding 200 cannon. The new castle cost the lives of about 20,000 men; ordered to drag huge guns up to the top of the mountain, the weary labourers steadily dropped to their knees one by one from sheer exhaustion, and Christophe had them executed on the spot. To prove the loyalty of his soldiers, Henry Christophe once paraded an entire squadron on a high castle parapet and marched them over the edge to certain death. Those who disobeyed were tortured and executed. When his people finally rebelled against him in 1820 he cheated a lynch mob by shooting his brains out.

To celebrate the birth of his first son, Francisco Solano Lopez, President of Paraguay, ordered a 101-gun salute, destroying eleven buildings in the process.

Bolivia has had more military coups than any other country in the world. In 1864 the ruling president Belzu addressed a large crowd from the balcony of the Palacio Quemado, to chants of 'Long live Belzu'. His soon-to-be successor, General Mariano Melgarejo, accompanied by a few men, entered the palace riding a horse. Shots were heard inside, then Melgarejo emerged on the balcony. He announced: 'Belzu is dead, who lives now?' The crowd responded: 'Long live Melgarejo'. Melgarejo was to be remembered as the most erratic of Bolivia's nineteenth-century despots. He once marched out of Bolivia at the head of a military expedition to support France's Emperor Napoleon III, but gave up and went home after a rainstorm and a terrible hangover impeded his progress. On another occasion he ceded territory to Brazil in exchange for a thoroughbred horse. When the British ambassador in La Paz declined an invitation to get drunk with him, Melgarejo lifted up his mistress's skirts and told the envoy to kiss her bare bottom. When the diplomat refused Melgarejo had him paraded through the capital, naked and facing backwards on a mule. Neither Queen Victoria nor her prime minister Viscount Palmerston were very amused, and 'Pam' ordered the immediate bombardment of Bolivia's landlocked capital by the Royal Navy. When informed that La Paz, 200 miles inland from the Pacific, was out of gunshot range, they contented themselves with having Bolivia erased from every British map instead.

Idi Amin once refused to attend the Commonwealth Games unless the Queen sent him a new pair of size-thirteen boots.

Nicolae Ceausescu bulldozed the centre of Bucharest, a city once known as the Paris of the Balkans, to make way for a monumental avenue, the Boulevard of Socialist Victory, leading to the world's largest palace, an architectural eyesore incorporating the work of around 700 interior designers, second in size only to the Pentagon, and featuring a marble-lined nuclear bunker. The construction of the new Palace of the People required the destruction of dozens of historic buildings, including twenty-six churches, and forced about 40,000 people to give up their homes in exchange for a small apartment in a grim, concrete residential block; thin interior walls and bugging devices were standard, drainage was not. The relocated masses were required to sign paperwork to request the demolition of their houses. Compensation for the lucky ones was a fraction of their actual worth; the less fortunate had to pay for the cost of demolition.

The North Korean leader Kim Il Sung, omnipresent even by the standards of cult dictatorship, had around seventy bronze statues and over 20,000 plaster busts made in his image. Every household was obliged to hang his portrait and the entire population of his country were compelled to wear lapel badges with his face on them. There were twenty different kinds of Kim Il Sung badges manufactured, worn according to class.

More than 90 per cent of the Chinese people wore Chairman Mao badges, each embossed with Mao Zedong's image; estimates of the total number produced range between 2.5 billion and 5 billion. Most carried the left profile of Mao's head, some showed full frontal views of his head or his body from the waist up, and on rare occasions his whole body. In deference to the prevailing political mood, badges featuring Mao's right profile were taboo. Each badge had a safety pin with which it could be affixed to clothing, or, for the more zealous, directly through the skin.

The Paraguayan dictator Alfredo Stroessner put up a neon sign in his nation's capital that proclaimed his magnificence twenty-four hours a day: 'Peace . . . Work . . . Well-being . . . Stroessner . . . Peace . . . Work . . . Well-being . . . Stroessner . . .'

Rafael Trujillo made certain that his Christ-like presence was felt in every corner of the Dominican Republic. As well as the 1,870 monuments erected to him, village water pumps bore signs reading 'Trujillo alone gives us water to drink', while homes for the aged had notices declaring 'Trujillo is the only one who gives us shelter'. The capital, formerly Santo Domingo, was renamed Ciudad Trujillo after the man himself, and there were neon signs throughout the city with the legend 'God and Trujillo'. Trujillo liked to collect bottle caps as a child and acquired the nickname *chapita*, slang for bottle cap. He always hated the nickname; as president he solved the problem by banishing the word from the language.

In 1978 Nicolae Ceausescu planned to make a welcome speech to new students of Bucharest's polytechnic. His chosen venue was the local park, but he was annoyed to find that where open parkland had once lain, a huge hole had been excavated to make way for Bucharest's new underground station. He simply ordered the hole to be 'removed' until after his speech. Throughout the night, hundreds of labourers toiled to fill in the hole, covering it with grass and trees uprooted from other parts of the city. Nobody told the civil engineer in charge of the Bucharest Metro project, who was most surprised when he turned up for work the following morning to find trees and park benches where his station should have been.

Colonel Joseph Mobutu took control of the Belgian Congo in 1965 and immediately launched an 'authenticity campaign' to break with his country's colonial past. Everything with a European name had to be renamed with a new African one – buildings, people, even the country itself, which became known as Zaire. He banned the wearing of Western-style clothing, and in a unique political fashion statement he declared a Mao-style suit, the *abacost*, the new national dress. Western forms of address such as 'Mr' and 'Mrs' were forbidden, and everyone was to be known as 'citizen'. Mobutu's propagandists had his portrait hung in every shop, bank and business, and depicted him on television every day riding a cushion of clouds. Mobutu spread official rumours about his alleged supernatural feats, including the lion he killed with his bare hands at the age of seven and the battle he fought against Zaire's enemies where bullets and spears bounced off his chest. He always carried a wooden walking stick featuring a carved eagle, a symbol of power that allegedly took the strength of eight normal men to carry. He was particularly keen that his countrymen knew about his sexual prowess; the new official title he took for himself was 'Sese Seko Kuku Ngbendu Wa Za Banga': 'The cock that leaves no hen unruffled'.

The President of Turkmenistan, Saparmurat Niyazov, is Asia's most ubiquitous despot. Towns, mosques, factories, power plants, universities, airports, brands of aftershave, vodka, yogurt, tea and even a meteor are named in honour of the self-styled Turkmenbashi (Father of all the Turks) whose features can be seen smiling down from every public building next to his Nazi-inspired slogan, '*Halk, Watan, Turkmenbashi*' ('Nation, People, Leader'). Turkmenistan's three state-sponsored television channels are vehicles for musical ensembles, whose performers, clad in traditional dress, spend part of each performance offering up praise for the life of their omnipresent president, his mother and his family. Niyazov personally commissioned a nineteen-part English-language TV soap opera, in which a Western woman moves to Turkmenistan and falls in love with the country, a series called, naturally, *Turkmenbashi, My Leader*. Among the hundreds of monuments to Turkmenbashi, the most conspicuous is a 120-foot golden statue in the capital, Ashgabat, erected on a motorized plinth. The monument rotates a full 360 degrees every twenty-four hours so that the president's arm always points to the sun, although some say that it's really the other way around. Every town in Turkmenistan has a Turkmenbashi Street; confusingly, Ashgabat has several. His image also adorns the nation's stamps and currency, causing a costly recall when his black hair turned white after a quadruple heart bypass operation in 2001. Although few of his countrymen are allowed to use it, Niyazov built an airport – Turkmenbashi International Airport – which is bigger than JFK, but with only three flights a day. Prior to an important visit by a foreign dignitary, jet airplanes are scrambled over the skies of Ashgabat, releasing gigantic explosions which are believed to scatter the clouds. In May 2000 the airport received its most distinguished visitor to date, the Russian President Vladimir Putin. The guest was said to be livid when, at the banquet in his honour, Niyazov deliberately dragged out proceedings, including forty-two toasts, well past midnight so he could boast that Mr Putin's visit had lasted two days.

On 24 April 1966 the Ethiopian Emperor Haile Selassie became one of the few foreign heads of state to consent to visit 'Papa Doc' Duvalier's Haiti. Preening himself as a world-class statesman, Papa Doc planned a massive and elaborate civic reception, 'borrowed' Haiti's few luxury cars, filled in all of the potholes on Port-au-Prince's main thoroughfare and renamed it Avenue Haile Selassie. Papa Doc was disappointed when his VIP declined an invitation to stay even for one night.

Nicolae Ceausescu specialized in large-scale, theatrical public spectacles designed to convince the Romanian people that they were living in a socialist paradise. Factory workers spent months rehearsing dance routines for stadium events at which thousands of people would line up to spell Ceausescu's name with their bodies – a real-life communist version of *Springtime for Hitler*. Meanwhile Romanian poets, intellectuals and journalists, knowing on which side their bread was buttered, fought each other in exhausting the dictionary to find the most impressive words to describe their leader and his First Lady Elena. He was routinely described as 'the greatest genius of the age', the 'guarantor of the nation's progress and independence', 'source of our light', 'the Danube of thought', 'builder of the outstanding stage in the millennia-old existence of the Romanian people', 'creator of the epoch of unprecedented renewal', 'treasure of wisdom and charisma' and 'the visionary architect of the nation's future'. The cult of Mrs Ceausescu, meanwhile, lagged only slightly behind that of her husband. On her sixtieth birthday, 6 January 1979, the press devoted dozens of pages to her, thanking the former seamstress for 'forty years of revolutionary activity' under such headlines as 'Great Example of Devotion and Revolutionary Passion', 'Leading Fighter of the Party for the Glorious Destiny of Romania' and 'Prestigious Contribution to the Evolution of Romanian Science, to the Cause for Peace and International Cooperation'. In 1980 she was accorded the new official preamble: 'Comrade academician doctor engineer Elena Ceausescu, brilliant politician and patriotic scholar of broad international renown'. Romania's workers were fed daily doses of patriotic pop songs dedicated to the presidential couple, sung by factory production-line bands. A popular favourite, 'Scientist of International Esteem', sung by the Chorus of the Savinesti Synthetic Fibre Factory featured the lyric: 'Comrade Elena Ceausescu / Great scientist of international esteem / In chemistry's noblest endeavours / We achieve our glorious communist dream'. Uniquely among twentieth-century despots, the Ceausescus had their own 'house style'. Romanian newspapers were required to mention the name of their leader no fewer than forty times on every page and always in their own special typeface. The names of Nicolae and his wife Elena had to be written on the same line; no other names could be quoted in the same paragraph, nor were they ever photographed against a blue background, only on red, the approved colour of the Communist revolution.

Enver Hoxha deployed schoolchildren to spell out party slogans on the Albanian hillsides in white painted stones. It was a gruelling and time-consuming exercise. Students who were well behaved had to maintain only simple, short slogans, such as 'Long Live Enver', 'Enver Party' and 'Albania: Rock of Granite'. Those who fell out of favour were punished with longer messages, including 'Up with Revolutionary Spirit', 'The Worst Enemy Is a Forgotten One' and 'American Imperialism Is Only a Paper Tiger'.

The North Korean leader Kim Il Sung, who had every road in the country built with an extra lane for his sole private use, never saw active military service. According to the official records, however, over a period of fifteen years he participated in more than 100,000 battles against the Japanese – an average of over twenty battles a day.

Benito Mussolini was inclined to take himself very seriously. In 1937 the English journalist Vernon Bartlett interviewed Il Duce, and when it was over he sent the draft to Mussolini's office to be vetted. As Bartlett recalled, the only alteration made to the manuscript was significant: 'Somewhere I had written, "The Duce's laughter encouraged me to ask another indiscreet question." The word "laughter" had been crossed out, and "cordiality" stood in its place. Apparently, no dictator may laugh.' Mussolini's grip on the Italian press also left little room for humour, especially comic strips, which the fascists considered alien to the Italian cultural tradition and a propaganda vehicle for Anglo-Saxon democracies. The only American cartoon hero not to be banned was Mickey Mouse – a big favourite with Mussolini's children. Mussolini also launched an anti-swearing campaign with a series of posters all over the country ordering '*Non bestemmiare per l'onore d'Italia*' ('Do not swear for the honour of Italy'). The only effect the notices had, however, was to encourage people to invent a new crop of oaths directed at Il Duce and his f**king posters.

Chairman Mao achieved a god-like respect among the Chinese peasantry. Presented with several watermelons by the Pakistani ambassador, he gave one to a village whose collective farm had performed well. The artefact was considered far too important to eat. Instead of sharing it out among themselves, the villagers put it on display, filling it with formaldehyde when it began to rot.

In 2003 Saparmurat Niyazov, President of Turkmenistan, initiated a national holiday in honour of the muskmelon, a relative of the watermelon, complete with lavish festivities in which everyone was obliged to take part. A spokesman on the state-owned national TV explained, 'This godsend has a glorious history.'

Idi Amin patented the word 'president' and banned anyone else in Uganda – including heads of companies, unions and other organizations – from using the title. Later he began calling himself 'King of Scotland', having already promoted himself to field marshal and awarded himself the VC. By the end of his reign in 1979, Amin had also adopted the title 'President for Life'. Whenever Ugandan newspapers wrote about him, however, they were obliged to accord him the full paragraph-long version: 'His Excellency, Field Marshal, Al-Haji, Dr Idi Amin Dada, Life President of Uganda, conqueror of the British Empire, distinguished service order of the Military Cross, Victoria Cross and Professor of Geography.' If there was one thing he enjoyed more than showering himself with titles, it was poking fun at the British by reversing the traditional images of colonialism. When he was elected chairman of the Organization of African Unity in 1975, the 21-stone despot arrived at the reception in Kampala carried on a sedan chair on the shoulders of four white businessmen; another white man kept time, holding a parasol, while the band struck up 'Colonel Bogey'.

Benito Mussolini, who was always shown in official portraits looking stony-faced and wearing military attire, personally vetted every picture taken of him before they appeared in the press. On the back of each photograph he scribbled either 'yes' or 'no' followed by a large 'M'. Those that showed Il Duce looking jovial or relaxed, rather than stern and straight-faced, were marked 'no'. Pictures of Mussolini with nuns or clergy were forbidden because he thought this would bring him bad luck. Any photograph that showed the potato-sized benign cyst on the back of his neck was similarly banned; any photographer who accidentally took a picture in which the cyst was visible would have his film completely destroyed.

Nicolae Ceausescu was an incredibly short man – not that the world would know it from the photographic evidence of his time in office. Photographs of Ceausescu meeting foreign dignitaries were always taken at a foreshortened angle so that he looked taller than, or at least as tall as, his guests. No such measures were necessary for domestic photo opportunities, however, as appointments to his government were often made on the basis of height. Ceausescu insisted that his ministers had to look up to him; consequently, two of his most senior ministers, Postelnicu and Bobu, were near dwarfs. The stock photos of Ceausescu in the 1980s also showed him looking twenty years younger and wrinkle-free ... the result of a great deal of retouching, which had occasionally bizarre results. In 1989 he was photographed meeting the Bulgarian dictator Zhivkrov, who was wearing a hat. As Ceausescu was hatless in the original photo, the retouchers were required to hastily paint in a hand holding a hat. Unfortunately they forgot to remove one of his real hands; Ceausescu appeared in the newspapers the following morning with three arms.

Josef Stalin was small and misshapen, born with webbed toes on his left foot and scarred by smallpox. Court artists were warned to favour his right profile because it bore fewer pockmarks. His shortness also rankled with him, causing him to wear platform heels in an effort to appear taller. Stalin chain-smoked cigarettes, but was often portrayed in photographs with the fingers of his left hand curled around a pipe. The pipe, an important part of his image, was a prop to disguise another deformity; when he was a child he was run over by a horse and cart, and as a result of his injuries suffered septicaemia, leaving him with a permanently crooked left arm.

Enver Hoxha once ordered the entire population of Tirana to stand in the rain without umbrellas so that he and his wife Nexhmije could drive around the city and enjoy the spectacle of a few hundred thousand people getting wet.

Although he was a regicide, Stalin liked to compare himself to the great Tsars of Russia, and joked that he might eventually marry a princess, a prospect that doubtless raised a few nervous smiles in the royal houses of Europe. Stalin once advised the Yugoslav dictator Tito to restore the King of Yugoslavia to the throne, adding, 'You can always stick a knife in his back when no one's looking.'

Joaquin Balaguer, the diminutive President of the Dominican Republic, bankrupted his country by spending millions on a massive illuminated cross, intended to commemorate the 500th anniversary of the arrival of Christopher Columbus in the Americas. Slums were razed to make way for the project, and escalating costs led to soaring food prices. Balaguer was forced to cancel the opening ceremony in 1990 when he was snubbed by his invited guests, the King of Spain and the Pope. When the illumination was finally switched on for the first time it caused a massive and disastrous drain on the national grid, which went unnoticed by the 60 per cent of his people who still did not have electricity. Balaguer kept the reins of power for twenty-two years thanks to blatant ballot-box fraud. The self-styled 'Dominican Nazarene' toured the countryside in a Popemobile-type vehicle with a glass tower, handing out gifts to peasants, ranging from sweets and bicycles to money and plots of land. He was elected seven times, the last three when he was almost completely blind, with the slogan, 'I will not be asked to thread needles while in office'. In 1996, blind, deaf and eighty-nine years old, Balaguer challenged a civil servant suspected of fraud to a duel, but changed his mind at the last minute and settled for a speech in parliament instead.

In 1870 Paraguay's President Francisco Lopez declared himself a Saint of the Christian Church. When the matter was put to the bishops of Paraguay, the twenty-three who did not agree were shot. 'Saint' Francisco was duly anointed and the date officially entered into the Christian calendar.

While presenting an image of a timid, bespectacled country doctor to the outside world, 'Papa Doc' Duvalier terrified the uneducated peasantry of Haiti by posing as the incarnation of a malevolent voodoo deity called Baron Samedi, guardian of the graveyard – but he also liked to compare himself to Jesus Christ. He instigated a graffiti campaign claiming 'Duvalier is God'. His best-known propaganda image showed Christ standing behind a seated Papa Doc with his right hand on the president's shoulder and featuring the caption 'I have chosen him'; a flashing neon sign erected outside his presidential palace proclaimed: 'I am the Haitian flag: I am indivisible'. In 1963 six Haitian students responded by painting 'Caca Doc' ('Doc is s**t') on a Port-au-Prince wall. Dozens of students and their relatives, including several university professors, were arrested and beaten; the six culprits were personally interrogated by the president in his basement room, then executed. Finally Papa Doc banned all youth organizations in Haiti, including the Boy Scouts. Although Papa Doc was an expert in violence and intimidation, his speciality was fraudulent election fixes. When his countrymen went to the polls in 1961 they found pre-printed at the top of each ballot sheet the words 'Doctor François Duvalier, President'. The votes were counted and it was announced that Papa Doc had been unanimously re-elected; after all, his name appeared on every ballot paper. A few years later he used a familiar tactic to prolong his stay in office ad infinitum: when Haitian voters were asked, 'Do you want your President elected for life?', the answer was a convenient and resounding 'yes'; apparently there wasn't room on the ballot sheet for a 'no' box.

The Belarusian president Alexander Lukashenko is considered the most gaffe-prone of the former Soviet state leaders. Although a quarter of his countrymen died during the Nazi occupation, 'Father Luke' confessed to being a huge admirer of Hitler's leadership qualities. In the face of overwhelming international condemnation he refused to retract his praise of the Führer, but admitted that the Nazis 'were bad on foreign policy'. Lukashenko was once irritated by the presence of a couple of dozen foreign ambassadors in Minsk and gave them a week's notice to vacate their residential complex for 'urgent plumbing repairs'. In case they didn't get the message, he had the gates welded shut. Lukashenko also shut down the biggest McDonald's in his capital and forbade the opening of any more outlets on the grounds that hamburgers were unhealthy. 'Father Luke' advised that they should be replaced with a new fast-food chain serving cabbage soup and fried mashed-potato pancakes.

Macias Nguema, dictator of Equatorial Guinea, who once gave his countrymen six months to give up their Christian names for African ones, underwent several transformations and by the end of his rule was known as Masie Nguema Biyogo Ñegue Ndong. In 1974 he ordered every Catholic priest in Equatorial Guinea to read the following message during Mass: 'Never without Macias, always with Macias. Down with colonialism and with ambition.' He had his own portrait displayed on every altar in every church, above the message: 'Only and unceasing miracle of Equatorial Guinea. God created Equatorial Guinea thanks to Macias. Without Macias, Equatorial Guinea would not exist.' A priest who refused to cooperate was later found frozen to death in a refrigeration truck.

From 1992–4 the North Korean authorities published over 300 poems and over 400 hymns in praise of their Dear Leader Kim Jong Il. Recent poems have paid tribute to Kim's skills as a cutting-edge gardener. He is said to have grown and nurtured a new flower, a hybrid orchid called *Kimjongilia*. According to the North Korean press, on Kim's birthday *Kimjongilia* has been known to miraculously bloom in the dead of winter.

The people of Turkmenistan are required to swear an oath of loyalty to President Saparmurat Niyazov that includes the line: 'If I criticize you, may my tongue fall out.' Their chief executive, however, alternates totalitarian ruthlessness and arbitrary oppression with token acts of kindness, for example, stopping his motorcade to distribute cash to children and randomly pardoning criminals. In 1993 he jailed his few remaining political opponents, but then abolished the death penalty and issued a blanket political amnesty after a bout with kidney disease caused a rethink. He explained: 'I had a bad dream about the death penalty. I think I was killing innocent people, so I'm not doing that any more.'

'Papa Doc' Duvalier had the Lord's Prayer rewritten for use in Haitian schools:

   'Our Doc, who art in the National Palace for life, hallowed be Thy name by present and future generations. Thy will be done in Port-au-Prince as it is in the provinces. Give us this day our new Haiti, and forgive not the trespasses of those anti-patriots who daily spit upon our country . . .'

Having already abolished ballet, theatre, circuses, loud mobile-phone conversations, music in cars, maths tuition in schools, gold teeth, beards and long hair on men, President Niyazov of Turkmenistan took everyone by surprise in 2002 by abolishing the calendar. He renamed the days of the week Bash Gun (Main Day), Yash Gun (Young Day), Hosh Gun (Good Day), Sogap Gun (Blessed Day), Anna (Friday), Rukh Gun (Spiritual Day) and Dynch Gun (Rest Day). The twelve months of the year were restyled after his country's heroes and most potent national symbols, thus January became Turkmenbashi (after himself) and April became simply Mother, after his dearly departed mum. Niyazov also issued a decree redefining youth and age. All Turkmen up to the age of twenty-five are officially 'adolescents'. People between the ages of twenty-five and thirty-seven are in their 'youth'; from forty-nine to sixty-one, 'prophetic'. The ages between sixty-two and seventy-three belong to the 'inspirational'. 'Old age' is conveniently postponed to eighty-five – another twenty-three years before Turkmen have to fret about retirement. People between the ages of ninety-seven and one hundred and nine are 'Oguzkhan', after the supposed father of the Turkmen nation. There is no word for those who outlive the system. Life expectancy for the average Turkmen male is sixty years.

From the day it became a republic in 1823 to the 'coronation' of the dictator Porfirio Diaz in 1876, Mexico had seventy-four different governments in fifty-three years, a wild and woolly period when a show of firearms could make anyone President For A Day – one such president, Victoriano Huerta, shot a man dead on the floor of the Mexican Senate for making a speech against him. One of the few Mexican chief executives who did not succumb to a fatal dose of lead poisoning was the hero of the Alamo, Antonio Lopez de Santa Anna. Surviving defeats, sex scandals, opium addiction and well-founded accusations of corruption, Santa Anna served as president of his country eleven times and lived to die in bed at the age of eighty-two. Santa Anna and his troops once found themselves near a wood known to be full of Texan soldiers, but as it was after midday they insisted on taking their usual siesta. While Santa Anna and his men quietly snoozed, the Texans attacked and routed the entire Mexican army in under twenty minutes. Santa Anna escaped, but two years later had a leg torn off in a skirmish with the French. He recovered the severed leg, and when he eventually became the most powerful man in Mexico, he gave the limb a full state funeral. At public events he took to riding on horseback waving his new cork leg over his head as a symbol of his sacrifices for his country. In 1847, again facing the United States at the Battle of Cerro Gordo in Mexico, Santa Anna was enjoying a quiet roast chicken lunch when his appetite was ruined by an uninvited regiment of Illinoisans, who stole his cork leg. Santa Anna hobbled away to fight another day but the iconic limb remained in American hands, despite many requests from the Mexican government to return it. In the 1850s army veterans charged a nickel or a dime for curiosity-seekers to handle the leg in hotel bars. Santa Anna's prosthesis, a trophy of war, now resides in the Guard's Museum, Camp Lincoln in Springfield, Illinois.

PROFILE: SAPARMURAT NIYAZOV

Born: 19 February 1940.

Also known as: Turkmenbashi (Father of all the Turks); the Moonlike Prophet.

Occupation: The First and Eternal President of Turkmenistan from 1991.

Hobbies: Building monuments; poetry – he previewed his collection of prose *The Three Evils Threatening Our Homeland* (those evils being indiscipline, arrogance and wayward thinking) on live TV, moments after sacking the commander-in-chief of the armed forces. Previous literary works include the epic *White Wheat*, dedicated to Turkmenistan's harvest and *Mother*, dedicated to his late mother.

Career highlight: Renamed the month of April and the word for 'bread' after his mother.

Career lowlight: Forced to quit smoking in 1997 after undergoing heart surgery – the entire population of Turkmenistan was obliged to follow suit.

Significant others: He is said to be obsessed with his deceased mother Gurbansoltan, who was killed by an earthquake in 1948 when he was eight.

Style: King of post-Soviet kitsch.

Whimsical cruelty factor:

Forces his countrymen to watch his private TV channel, which has no foreign news, only traditional singing and dancing, and all-day readings of Niyazov's poems.

Legacy: Monuments; at least 20,000 people sent to labour camps; more monuments.

Wit and wisdom: 'I watched young dogs when I was young. They were given bones to gnaw. Those of you whose teeth have fallen out did not gnaw bones. This is my advice.' – dispensing tips on oral hygiene to the young people of Turkmenistan in 2004.

Born: 24 July 1827.

Died: 1 March 1870.

Also known as: El Mariscal.

Occupation: President of Paraguay 1862–70.

Hobbies: Womanizing and gluttony – 'a tidal wave of human flesh' was one of the more flattering descriptions of his ample form. In constant pain from his rotten teeth, he routinely sought relief by quaffing industrial quantities of brandy.

Career highlight: One hundred years after his death, during the dictatorship of General Alfredo Stroessner, he was restored and celebrated as a National Hero.

Career lowlight: At the battle of Cerro Cora in 1870, he lost an ear to a Brazilian souvenir hunter.

Significant others: Courtesan mistress Eliza Lynch, variously known as 'Madame Lynch' and 'the Irish whore'.

Style: The Napoleon of the South Americas; owned several wardrobes full of outlandish military costumes, worn so tight he could barely walk.

Whimsical cruelty factor: 🖐 🖐 🖐 🖐

He had two of his sisters put in cages, occasionally allowing them out but only to be flogged; ordered the assassination of his own mother.

Legacy: Killed and tortured thousands who opposed him; launched the suicidal War of the Triple Alliance, which reduced Paraguay's pre-war population of 525,000 by 60 per cent. Only 28,000 survivors were men.

CHAPTER 5
Stand By Your Mao: Leaders' Wives

Jiang Qing, the Shanghai actress who became the third wife of Chairman Mao, was one of China's most powerful and reviled figures, the Yoko Ono of contemporary Chinese politics. As one of the radical Gang of Four, Jiang spearheaded persecutions during the Cultural Revolution, tyrannizing her political enemies and brutalizing China's artists and intellectuals. Madame Mao, however, had a soft spot for Western tearjerkers. One of the Cultural Revolution's victims was Shi Xianrong, a translator of Arthur Miller, who was demoted to pig farming in the gulag. He was later rescued from penury and summoned to appear before Madame Mao, where he discovered to his astonishment that his task was to be a private translation of Erich Segal's *Love Story*. Later he translated *Jonathan Livingston Seagull* for her.

Imelda Marcos, wife and confidante of the Philippine dictator Ferdinand Marcos, experienced a 'mystical vision' which prompted her to spend $100 million on an attempt to create a Philippine version of the Cannes film festival. Most of the money was spent on an extravagant new film theatre. The builders and everyone else associated with the Marcos family were so corrupt that no one was particularly surprised when, two months before the official opening in 1982, half of the building collapsed, killing at least thirty workers. To avoid delaying construction she had concrete poured over the dead men and had the theatre exorcized to appease the superstitious. The grand opening went ahead almost exactly as Imelda had planned, with just one minor setback: she had invited the Pope, but in the event had to settle for Brooke Shields.

Among the first Red Army soldiers to penetrate Hitler's bunker on 2 May 1945 were a dozen women from a medical unit, who wanted to help themselves to Eva Braun's clothes.

Before she became Romania's First Lady, Elena Ceausescu held a variety of unskilled jobs, including a brief spell as a hired hand in a back-street laboratory producing slimming and headache pills. Her lab experience came in useful years later when her husband Nicolae appointed her chairman of ICECHIM, the main chemistry research laboratory in Romania. Almost as mysteriously, she acquired a doctorate in chemistry – a remarkable achievement for someone who had left school with only a certificate in needlework – and a new official title; from now on she was to be introduced in all communications as 'Elena Ceausescu, world-renowned chemist and scientist'. Most of her official trips abroad were excuses to acquire honorary degrees in recognition of her 'scientific work'. The Romanian foreign office was instructed to negotiate with the most distinguished academic institutions in whatever country the Ceausescus were planning to visit, to seek awards for Elena, along with a hint that the couple might cancel their trip if an award was not forthcoming. Before her official visit to Britain in 1978, Oxford and Cambridge universities and the Fellowship of the Royal Society were approached and asked if they would like to give Madame Ceausescu an honorary degree. The petitions were politely turned down, although she was delighted to receive honorary degrees from both Central London Polytechnic and the Royal Institute of Chemistry. She was less impressed in 1978 when she went to the United States. As no Washington-based academy was prepared to acknowledge Elena's scientific achievements, she was offered membership of the Illinois Academy of Science. She grudgingly took the award on offer, complaining that she had never heard of Illinois, and was put out at having to accept such a 'low-ranked' degree from the hands of a 'dirty Jew' (Dr Emanuel Merdinger was head of the Illinois Academy of Science). To keep up appearances as a 'brilliant scientist of world renown', the writings of many genuine Romanian scientists were often published under her name. She once complained that she had never been nominated for the Nobel Prize in chemistry, despite her many publications.

In 1974 Idi Amin divorced three of his four wives and ordered them out of his home. He was incensed when one of his ex-wives, Kay, was later found dead in her apartment after a clumsy abortion attempt. Amin took her six-year-old son to see her in the mortuary. When they arrived they found that her head was back to front, her legs had been sewn on to her shoulders and her arms attached to her pelvis. Amin explained: 'This what happen to bad women.'

Imelda Marcos had an entire palace ballroom converted into a karaoke hall for her to lip-synch pop songs in, but there were no Lennon/McCartney numbers in her repertoire. In 1966 The Beatles went to play a concert in Manila and, on a tight schedule and expecting a quick getaway, they politely declined an invitation to take tea with the First Lady. Furious at the snub, Imelda withdrew the security assigned to the Fab Four, leaving them at the mercy of thousands of hostile Filipinos, protesting against the perceived discourtesy, booing, kicking and jostling them as they left their hotel, before battering the band's getaway limousine all the way back to the airport. Imelda enforced a ban on Beatles' records in the Philippines.

Female news presenters on Romanian TV were forbidden to wear jewellery lest they appeared more glamorous than their First Lady, Elena Ceausescu. She also ordered a TV blackout after 10 p.m. so that the workers of Romania could wake up early in the morning, fresh to start a new day's work in order to complete the five-year plan.

Nigeria's military dictator Sani Abacha, who enjoyed hanging his critics while videotaping the executions for his personal viewing pleasure, stole more than $4 billion during his five-year reign. Abacha died of a heart attack in 1998, aged fifty-four, during a Viagra-fuelled romp with three Indian prostitutes. A few weeks after his death, police at Kano airport became suspicious when his widow, Maryam, tried to leave the country with thirty-eight pieces of luggage. Each was found to be stuffed with US dollars. Mrs Abachi explained she was not stealing the money, just 'putting away the funds in some foreign accounts for safe keeping'. To dispel any lingering suspicions that she may have had anything to hide, she hired the services of O. J. Simpson's legal expert Johnny Cochran.

In addition to her reputation as a world-class buyer of fashion footwear, Imelda Marcos was also said to be the world's single biggest buyer of jewellery. She had stores opened at night for private nocturnal showings, her bodyguards paying for her gems with thousand-dollar bills stashed in paper bags. As she always insisted on a discount, shop owners put their prices up by 25 per cent as soon as they knew she was coming, then offered her 15 per cent off. In addition to the 1,200 pairs of shoes that the Philippine government eventually confiscated from Imelda, they also took her only bulletproof bra.

Eva, second wife of the Argentinian President Juan Perón, died of cancer in 1952 at the age of thirty-three. By the time of her death, the eminent Spanish pathologist Dr Pedro Ara had been on standby for a fortnight to embalm her. With Eva barely cold, he filled her veins first with alcohol then glycerine, which kept her organs intact and made her skin appear almost translucent. Juan Perón planned to have her housed in a giant new mausoleum, but in 1955 he was forced to flee the country hurriedly. Eva's embalmed body was confiscated by the Argentinian military, who feared that it would become a rallying point for Peronists. For several years the corpse was moved from place to place, and copies were made out of wax, vinyl and fibreglass to throw Eva's followers off the trail. Her kidnapper Colonel Moori Koenig was known to display the body to his friends and to handle it; Eva's sister later hinted at more sinister goings-on, saying only, 'There are some things that should not be spoken of.' In 1971, however, Juan and Eva were touchingly reunited, although by now her nose was broken, a fingertip and one of her ears were missing, and her feet were mysteriously coated in tar. The corpse was ever-present in an open casket at the Perón family dinner table, alongside his new wife Isabelita, who apparently liked to comb Eva's hair.

Idi Amin met his future wife Sarah Kyolaba Amin, known as Suicide Sarah, while she was serving as a teenage go-go dancer with his army's Revolutionary Suicide Mechanized Regiment Band. The head of her then fiancé, Jesse Gitta, became one of many stored in the refrigerator of Amin's 'Botanical Room'. Idi and Sarah's wedding banquet in 1975 cost £2 million, and was attended by the best man, Palestinian leader Yasser Arafat, who was then regarded as an international pariah. Sarah left Amin in 1982 and sought political asylum in Germany, where she spent time as a lingerie model, then moved to London, running a café serving African dishes including goat stew and cow hoof in gravy. In 1999 environmental health officers closed down her establishment when they found a 'grey furry thing' in her kitchen. It was later identified as a decomposing mouse.

Elena Ceausescu employed the Romanian secret police to film the sexual liaisons of foreign diplomats, using these tapes to blackmail them. According to the Romanian chief of intelligence, she also had her own daughter Zoia on tape.

President Mobutu of Zaire slept with the wives of his government ministers and officials, both to humiliate his underlings and 'to keep an eye on things'. After the death of his first wife, Mobutu married his mistress, with whom he already had several children, then took her identical twin sister as his new mistress. No one could tell them apart, except possibly Mobutu. He said he kept twins as lovers to ward off malignant influences from his first wife's spirit.

The thirty-sixth US President Lyndon Baines Johnson, by reputation a distant second in the White House adultery stakes behind the man he replaced, was said to have 'the instincts of a Turkish Sultan'. LBJ was genuinely aggrieved that John F. Kennedy's reputation as a stud was somewhat greater than his own and complained to friends, 'I've had more women by accident than he has had on purpose.' The Philippine President Ferdinand Marcos was once informed by his wife Imelda that she was being groped by LBJ on the White House dance floor. Marcos replied, 'Ignore it, Meldy. It's in a good cause.'

Chairman Mao was once asked what would have happened if Khrushchev had been assassinated instead of President Kennedy in 1963. 'Well, I'll tell you one thing,' said Mao, 'Aristotle Onassis wouldn't have married Mrs Khrushchev.'

Born: Ferdinand Edralin Marcos on 11 September 1917.

Died: 28 September 1989.

Occupation: President of the Republic of the Philippines 1965–86.

Hobbies: Pocketing generous handouts from the World Bank.

Career highlights: Political career got off to a flying start at the age of twenty-one when he shot dead his father's victorious opponent in the Philippines' elections; despite his record as a murderer (and a Nazi sympathizer), he was elected President of the Philippines in 1965. Repeated his party trick in 1983 when exiled chief opposition leader Benigno Aquino returned to the Philippines; Aquino was shot in the head as he stepped out on to the tarmac at Manila International Airport.

Career lowlight: One of history's greatest kleptocrats, he fled the country in 1986, and was later indicted by the US on racketeering charges.

Significant others: Former beauty queen wife Imelda (Miss Manila 1958) who, according to a US Senator, 'made Marie Antoinette look like a bag lady'.

Family: Children Imee Marcos-Manotoc, Ferdinand 'Bong-bong' Marcos and Irene Marcos-Araneta.

Style: So vain he had his face carved into a mountainside, á la Mount Rushmore.

Whimsical cruelty factor: 🥊 🥊 🥊

He had his enemies' heads slammed into walls, and their genitals and pubic hair torched.

Legacy: His rampant corruption left the Philippines with a foreign debt of £26 billion – of which at least £6 billion went into Marcos's Swiss bank accounts.

Wit and wisdom: 'They went into my closets looking for skeletons, but thank God all they found were shoes.' – wife Imelda Marcos.

PROFILE: JUAN PERÓN

Born: Juan Domingo Perón on 8 October 1895.

Died: 1 July 1974.

Also known as: El Lider.

Occupation: President of Argentina 1946–55, 1973–4.

Hobbies: Throwing house parties for the most notorious Nazi war criminals – the 'Angel of Death', Dr Josef Mengele, was allowed to live so freely under Perón's protection that he was listed in the Buenos Aires phonebook.

Career highlight: Swept to power in 1946 after addressing a mass rally of 300,000 'shirtless ones'.

Career lowlight: Sharing a dinner table with the corpse of his deceased wife Eva.

Significant others: Wives Eva Duarte ('Evita') and Isabelita.

Style: Sharp suits and dazzling good looks caused ladies at Peronist rallies to flash their panties and scream that they wanted to bear his children.

Whimsical cruelty factor: 👢 👢 👢 👢

An expert torturer whose methods combined medieval-style crudity with twentieth-century innovation. His death squads employed genital mutilations, gang rapes, skin peeling, burning with hot coals and acids, and immersion in water fouled with human waste. Repertoire included the 'telephone', an electric prod attached simultaneously to the mouth and ears; the 'helmet of death', an electrode-studded device placed on the victim's head; electrode-studded underwear; and the 'picana', a 12,000-volt electrical device attached to nipples, sexual organs and the soles of the feet, causing unbearable pain (and sterility) without trace – the body of the victim was always doused with water first for better conductivity.

Legacy: Escalating turmoil, terrorist activity and political violence; awful musical, stage play and film called *Evita*.

Wit and wisdom: 'Answer a violent action with another action still more violent.'

CHAPTER 6
Dictation:
The Despotic Muse

Adolf Hitler wrote his autobiography to cash in on the publicity stirred up by his trial and imprisonment for his part in the Beer Hall Putsch in 1924. Originally called *Four and a Half Years of Struggle Against Lies, Stupidity and Cowardice*, the manuscript was badly written and rambling. The first publisher he contacted turned it down flat, describing it as 'a veritable chaos of banalities, schoolboy reminiscences, subjective judgements and personal hatred'. An acquaintance suggested he change the title to the pithier *Mein Kampf*, and it went on to become a runaway bestseller, translated into sixteen languages and earning its author millions from royalties. Thoughtfully, there was also a Braille version for the blind.

Benito Mussolini published over forty-four volumes in and out of office, including a bodice-ripper *The Cardinal's Mistress*, and a critique of the Russian novel. In his final idle moments, before he was strung upside down by piano wire, Il Duce was translating Giosuè Carducci's *Odi Barbare* into German.

Mao Zedong's 'little red book', *The Thoughts Of Chairman Mao* – a collection of tips on such diverse subjects as farming, women and the need to keep up with one's grenade-throwing practice – is one of the world's all-time bestsellers, with the estimated number in print well exceeding 1 billion. The book's phenomenal success was partly due to the fact that it was an unofficial requirement for every Chinese citizen to own, read and carry it at all times; the punishment for failing to produce the book on demand ranged from being beaten to a pulp on the spot by Red Guards, to several years' hard labour.

'Papa Doc' Duvalier wanted to be recognized as a great writer on a par with political theorists such as Marx, Trotsky and Mao. In 1967 the Haitian dictator published his *Essential Works*, an imitation of Mao's 'little red book' right down to the red cover. Disappointed by poor sales, Papa Doc deducted $15 from the salary of all of Haiti's civil servants and in return the workers each received a copy of his book.

Libya's Colonel Muammar Gaddafi wrote *The Green Book*, a work of political theory, which was received by one Western critic as 'the sort of thing a fifteen-year-old might write under the title "My plan to reform the world"'. Gaddafi has also tried his hand at writing fiction; *Escape to Hell* is his collection of short stories and essays. One tale tells of an astronaut who returns to earth but cannot find work as a carpenter, plumber etc. because he lacks the necessary skills, so he kills himself. Another article discusses whether death is male or female. The introduction, supplied by Pierre Salinger, press secretary to the late President Kennedy, describes the book as 'fascinating – the work of an original mentality'.

Saddam Hussein commissioned a court calligrapher to reproduce a copy of Islam's holy book, the Koran, written entirely with Saddam's blood. The book is 605 pages long and took three years and fifty pints of blood, donated at a pint a time.

The Paraguayan strongman Alfredo Stroessner is the world's only dictator to have had a popular dance named after him. He gave the world 'the General Stroessner Polka'.

The published works of Enver Hoxha ran to thirty-nine volumes, including transcripts of his speeches, which although infamously long and tedious were seldom lacking in candour. The president began his keynote New Year message to the Albanian people in 1967: 'This year will be harder than last year,' adding, 'It will, however, be easier than next year.' Hoxha, who considered the Soviet Union too 'soft', spent his last few years as a total recluse, dictating dense, rambling books lambasting his communist allies for betraying the Marxist cause. His final book, *The Dangers of Anglo-Americans in Albania*, warned his countrymen to watch out for men with beards, which he believed were cunning devices used to disguise British and American spies.

Whenever Stalin mispronounced a word or a name in one of his speeches, his underlings always repeated the mistake – no one ever dared correct him. In 1936 the Soviet film chief Shumiatsky was granted permission to record a Stalin speech for a gramophone record. When his officials listened to the recording for the first time, they were horrified to find that the quality was far from perfect; there were background noises, gaps and jumps – there was also an anxious discussion about their leader's voice, which sounded distinctly 'tinny'. A government report concluded that something sinister had happened at the recording plant and that saboteurs had deliberately wrecked Stalin's voice. The NKVD were sent in and the guilty were punished.

Macias Nguema, the first president of Equatorial Guinea, was said to be deeply insecure about his lack of educational achievements and intellectual ability. He had everyone who wore spectacles murdered, as spectacles equalled short sight, and short sight was proof of intelligence and having read too much. In spite of sensitivity about his own literary skills, Nguema was the unwitting inspiration for a popular classic. In 1970 *The Times* reported that the novelist Frederick Forsyth had put up a quarter of a million dollars to fund a coup against Nguema, employing twelve British mercenaries and fifty soldiers from Biafra. The 'plot' was blown when one of the mercenaries shot himself after a gunfight with London police. Forsyth denied any participation in the plot and said he was only researching a book; the resulting 'fictional' work, *The Dogs of War*, was a bestseller.

In 1973 the French film director Barbet Schroeder persuaded Idi Amin to star in a documentary, *General Idi Amin Dada: A Self Portrait*. Schroeder was attracted to his subject by news reports that Amin enjoyed sending telegrams to various world leaders, including some to Queen Elizabeth addressing her as 'Liz', and one to Richard Nixon wishing him a 'speedy recovery' from Watergate. Another Amin telegram sent to UN Secretary General Kurt Waldheim in 1972 noted, 'Hitler was right about the Jews'. One of the highlights of the Schroeder documentary was a filmed cabinet meeting, during which Amin dictated policy while his ministers slavishly copied down his every word: 'Anybody found is a spy, his case must be dealt with by military tribunal. Even military tribunal should not waste time of making law all day discussing about one person who is a spy. Must be shortcut!' Amin also laid down rules, including, 'Miss three meetings and you're kicked out of government'. 'Big Daddy' was not happy with the finished documentary, and threatened the safety of French citizens living in his country unless the director trimmed two minutes and twenty-one seconds from it. Schroeder made the requested cuts, but restored the footage six years later when Amin was exiled.

North Korea's Dear Leader Kim Jong Il maintains a close personal interest in the film industry and once wrote a book, *Cinema and the Art of Directing*. The Pyongyang studio receives regular visits from their Leader, who issues artistic tips displayed on huge billboards. These tips range from the general to the specific. One note read, 'make more cartoons'. In others he explains to actors how to laugh, how to cry, and how to be good citizens at home. An actor who is going to play a football player, Kim explained, 'should actually become a football player himself and run sweating across the pitch to kick the ball.' Kim had a long-held ambition to make a Korean version of *Godzilla*. To realize his vision, in 1978 he kidnapped a noted South Korean film producer Shin Sang-ok and his wife, the actress Choe Eun-hui, so they could teach him how to make films. When the diminutive Kim met the actress for the first time he asked, 'Well, Madame Choe, what do you think of my physique? Small as a midget's turds, aren't I?' With the help of the reluctant director and his wife, Kim went on to make the epic *Pullgesari*, about a metal-eating monster who saves fourteenth-century Korean peasants from the tyranny of an evil warlord. It was seen outside the country for the first time in 1998 when it became an instant cult classic.

Saddam Hussein demonstrated his shy, sensitive side by penning anonymous romantic novels. He wrote (or more likely, employed a team of professionals to ghost-write) two books; the first, *Zabibah and the King*, became an instant bestseller upon its publication in 2000, a patriotic parable about a benign despot who falls in love with a beautiful woman married to a brutish, vicious husband. One chapter features the rape of the woman, which occurs on 17 January, coincidentally the day US and coalition forces launched the first Gulf War. The second novel, *The Fortified Castle*, was published in 2001, but did not sell well until Saddam's son Uday bought 250,000 copies. A third, unfinished work of fiction was due out just before he was forced into hiding.

PROFILE: MAO ZEDONG (TSE-TUNG)

Born: 26 December 1893.

Died: 9 September 1976.

Also known as: Chairman Mao; The Great Helmsman.

Occupation: Chairman of the People's Republic of China 1949–76.

Hobbies: Swimming and recreational sex, both well into his eighties.

Career highlight: In 1968 he banned *The Sound of Music*, describing it as 'a blatant example of capitalist pornography'.

Career lowlight: He was over-filled with embalming fluid in 1976, almost causing his head to burst.

Significant others: Jiang Qing ('Madame Mao').

Style: Regulation grey military-style 'Mao suit', previously known as the Sun Yat-sen suit. When Mao's outfit made its first appearance in 1949, his chief of protocol Yu Yinqing suggested in future that he keep to the more conventional dark suit when receiving foreign dignitaries. Yu's fashion tip went unheeded; he was fired and later committed suicide.

Whimsical cruelty factor:

Encouraged members of his Red Guard to eat the flesh of their enemies to show that they were fully class-conscious.

Legacy: Killed more people than Stalin and Hitler combined; 14 to 20 million deaths from starvation during the 'Great Leap Forward' and tens of thousands killed and millions of lives ruined during the 'Cultural Revolution' – now officially classified as 'mistakes', committed when Mao was old and no longer in control of his faculties.

Wit and wisdom: 'Apart from their other characteristics, the outstanding thing about China's 600 million people is that they are poor and blank.'

Born: 16 February 1941, his birth having been foretold by a swallow from heaven, and attended by a bright star and double rainbows.

Also known as: Dear Leader; Unprecedented Great Man; Bright Star of the Country; Guiding Focus; Genius of the Cinema; one half of the 'Axis of Evil'; Shorty.

Occupation: Supreme Leader of North Korea from 1997.

Hobbies: Asia's biggest collector of pornography; maintains a harem of around 2,000 imported blondes and young Asian women – the 'Joy Brigade' comprising a 'satisfaction team' for sexual favours, a 'happiness team' for massages and a 'dancing team' for post-coital karaoke and dancing performances.

Career highlights: Enjoying a personality cult beyond Mao's wildest dreams, lauded as all-round great soldier, peerless film-maker, movie critic, philosopher, scientist, brilliant and industrious scholar imbued with great wisdom etc. According to Pyongyang media reports, Kim has also learned how to 'expand space and shrink time' – a rare gift in a man who is afraid to fly or even board an aircraft.

Significant others: Deceased father Kim Il Sung who holds the post of 'Eternal Leader', but one of his many accomplishments – he once turned sand into rice, and could cross rivers on a leaflet. Both Kims are said to be descended from Tangun, a divine 'bear-man' who founded their country more than 5,000 years ago.

Style: The Asian Austin Powers.

Whimsical cruelty factor: 🧤🧤

Suffering from an irrational fear of triplets (three is a highly significant number to Koreans and triplets are revered as people who will rise to positions of power and influence), Kim ordered the seizure of all of his country's triplets and placed them in state-run orphanages after being tipped off that a triplet was destined to overthrow his regime. He also sanctioned the murder of babies born in camps to political prisoners.

Legacy: Ongoing, including a catastrophic famine that has killed millions of North Koreans since 1995.

CHAPTER 7
Sporting Dictators

Although he gained his country's presidency through the ballot box, by 1937 the Dominican leader Rafael Trujillo was ruling as an iron-fisted dictator, in control of the army and placing family members into high political office. The only thing he did not yet control was baseball, his country's national obsession. Trujillo decided to form his own baseball team, then dedicated the national baseball league to his re-election; there was more than sporting pride at stake. As his political opponents already owned a share in two other major teams in the Dominican League, for the dictator not to have the best baseball team in the country would have been an unacceptable loss of face. Trujillo took over two of the existing biggest rival teams and merged them to form one squad, the Ciudad Trujillo Dragons, then improved it by raiding the black American leagues for their most talented players. The climax of a tense season came when Trujillo's all-star side were forced into a dramatic seventh and deciding game of the championship series against a Cuban side, Estrellas de Oriente. On the eve of the big game, Trujillo tipped the odds in his favour by having some of the opposition squad thrown into jail, then let it be known to his own all-star team that their lives depended on a favourable result. When Trujillo's team entered the stadium the next day they found their employer's troops lined up with rifles and bayonets near the first base. The Dragons took the hint, won the series and Trujillo was comfortably re-elected by his baseball-mad countrymen. Trujillo was not the only Latin-American dictator to identify baseball with national pride. The Nicaraguan leader Anastasio Somoza once fired the Nicaraguan manager in the middle of a game in disgust and went into the dugout to direct operations himself.

Mussolini liked to show off his physical fitness by jogging down the lines when reviewing his troops, and he enjoyed humiliating out-of-shape visitors by making them run to his desk in the Palazzo Venezia and then run out again at the double, before saluting him from the door. Mussolini was also an enthusiastic, but poor, tennis player, which presented certain problems for his opponents. The Italian foreign minister Count Galeazzo Ciano noted that it took more skill and stamina to lose to Il Duce than it did to defeat most men. Hitler, on the other hand, by his own Aryan ideals was puny and not at all athletic. Unlike Mussolini, who loved to pose topless, the Führer was terrified of being seen without his clothes on, even by his valet, and never wore shorts because he was ashamed of his white knees. Whenever Hitler went for a walk at his favourite Bavarian retreat it was only ever downhill, and there was always a car at the bottom waiting to take him back up.

Nicolae Ceausescu loved hunting, but sportsmanship was not his style. The Romanian president was a poor shot and nearly always bagged less than anyone else in his shooting party. To compensate, his aides brought supplies of dead game and hung it outside his hunting lodge. Ceausescu mostly enjoyed shooting bears. Teams of forest rangers would spend hours preparing an area for a bear hunt, tying down half of a dead horse near a watering hole. When a large hungry bear arrived on the scene, the rangers would notify their president. Ceausescu would arrive by helicopter and depart with a bearskin a couple of hours later.

Idi Amin was heavyweight boxing champion of Uganda from 1951 until 1960. When his country was being overrun by Tanzanian troops in 1978, he suggested that he and Tanzanian President Julius Nyere settle the war between them in the ring, with Muhammad Ali as referee.

In 1956 Chairman Mao's Physical Culture and Sports Commission recognized a new track-and-field event, the hand-grenade throw.

Under the puritanical General Ne Win, Burma became one of the world's least tourist-friendly destinations. Visitors were not allowed to stay for more than twenty-four hours, which was perhaps just as well as the entire country had fewer hotel rooms than the Las Vegas Hilton. Neon signs and even Coca-Cola were unknown, as indeed were nightclubs, gambling and beauty contests. Curiously, Ne Win also banned horse racing, although he was known to be a regular at Ascot.

Idi Amin organized basketball games in which he alone was allowed to score. He once had a palace guard killed for blocking his shot.

King Carol II of Romania insisted on picking his country's football team for the 1930 World Cup Finals, where they beat Peru 3–1, and narrowly failed to reach the semi-finals by going out to the hosts and eventual winners, Uruguay. History will remember King Carol as a dangerous, power-mad despot – but one whose record in competitive international football was much better than that of England managers Graham Taylor and Kevin Keegan.

Saddam Hussein appointed his son Uday as head of both Iraq's Olympic committee and the Iraqi football federation; an inspired choice designed to give his nation's top athletes an extra incentive to do well. Those who did not perform up to expectations were beaten with iron bars, had the soles of their feet caned, and were dunked in raw sewage to ensure the wounds became infected. Motivational football team-talks included threats to cut off players' legs and throw them to ravenous dogs. A missed training session was punishable by imprisonment. A loss or a draw brought flogging with electric cable, or a bath in raw sewage. A penalty miss carried the certainty of imprisonment and torture. During a World Cup qualifying match in Jordan, Iraq drew 3–3 against the United Arab Emirates, resulting in a penalty shoot-out, which Iraq lost. Two days after the team returned to Baghdad, the captain Zair was summoned to Uday's headquarters, then blindfolded and taken away to a prison camp for three weeks. A red card was particularly dangerous. Yasser Abdul Latif, accused of thumping the referee during a heated club match in Baghdad, was confined to a prison cell two metres square, where he was stripped to the waist, then ordered to perform press-ups for two hours while guards flogged him with lengths of electric cable. When Iraq lost 4–1 to Japan in the Asian Cup, goalkeeper Hashim Hassan, defender Abdul Jaber and striker Qahtan Chither were fingered as the main culprits and were whipped for three days by Uday's bodyguards. When Iraq failed to reach the 1994 World Cup Finals, Uday made the squad train with a concrete football.

Idi Amin once phoned the Egyptian President Anwar Sadat to tell him that he wanted to become the world's first head of state to swim across the Suez Canal.

PROFILE: SADDAM HUSSEIN

Born: Saddam Hussein Al-Tikriti on 28 April 1947.

Also known as: Great Uncle; Anointed One; Glorious Leader; Direct Descendant of the Prophet; one half of the 'Axis of Evil'.

Occupation: President of Iraq, Chairman of the Iraqi Revolutionary Command Council 1979–2003.

Hobbies: A keen fisherman, but with little time for the subtleties of angling; he preferred to lob hand-grenades into the water, then have a diver pick up the dead fish.

Career highlights: Hiding those Weapons of Mass Destruction; being called 'the world's most evil man' by George W. Bush.

Career lowlights: (1) As a daring young Ba'ath party activist he attempted to shoot the Iraqi prime minister Abdul Kareem Qassem, but failed and shot himself in the foot instead; (2) A former mistress revealed that he secretly dyed his hair black and regularly used a 'relaxation mask' to reduce wrinkles; (3) Cowering in a spider hole before gratefully surrendering to a US soldier in 2003.

Significant others: Wives Sajida and Samira.

Family: Five children, including the delinquent Uday, famous for his flamboyant apparel, including his penchant for large bow ties, suits in colours to match his luxury cars, cowboy hats and beach shirts. Few passed comment on his dress sense; one employee had his tongue cut out after noting that Uday's multi-coloured shirts were 'a bit effeminate'.

Style: Dressed to kill and often did. Although not quite in the same league as Imelda Marcos, he had a passion for expensive footwear, the indulgence of a man who had gone barefoot as a peasant boy. In one year he killed three guards because they tried to steal some of his shoes. He and George W. Bush once owned three identical pairs of black, crocodile-leather shoes made by the Italian designer Vito Antioli.

Whimsical cruelty factor:

Shot a political enemy in public and sent the remains home in a shopping bag.

Legacy: Ongoing; up to 2 million dead as a result of three wars, an unknown number of dissidents killed and an estimated 500,000 Iraqi children dead because of trade sanctions.

Wit and wisdom: 'The great, the jewel and the mother of battles had begun.' – at the start of the 1991 Gulf War.

PROFILE: BENITO MUSSOLINI

Born: 29 July 1883.

Died: 28 April 1945.

Also known as: Il Duce; Musso the Wop.

Occupation: Prime Minister of Italy 1922–43.

Hobbies: A taste for sports cars, aeroplanes, and an endless succession of mistresses.

Career highlights: Invading Ethiopia. And Abyssinia.

Career lowlight: Strung upside down by piano wire in a Milanese square in April 1945.

Significant others: Wife Rachele, long-standing mistress Claretta Petacci.

Family: Sons, Vittorio and Romano, daughter Edda.

Style: Eclectic; for his famous march on Rome (actually a train ride), he wore a bowler hat, starched collar, jodhpurs and white spats.

Whimsical cruelty factor: 🐦🐦

The first twentieth-century despot to make torture official state policy; his blackshirts pumped their opponents full of castor oil to 'purge them of the will to live': victims usually choked to death.

Legacy: Although a distant third on the scale of Second World War dictators, he was still responsible for the deaths of over 400,000 Italians and at least 30,000 Ethiopians.

Wit and wisdom: 'This is the epitaph I want on my tomb: "Here lies one of the most intelligent animals who ever appeared on the face of the earth".'

CHAPTER 8
Private Dictators

Chairman Mao disliked most things western, especially toilets with a seat and flushing mechanism, and always refused to use them, even when he was abroad. When he went to Moscow, he insisted on squatting over a bedpan because all the toilets in the Kremlin were of the flushing variety. Mao's bowel movements were a daily topic of conversation in the highest echelons of the Chinese government. He was so severely constipated that one of his bodyguards had to administer an enema every three days, and a normal movement was a cause for celebration among his top officials.

Benito Mussolini was very careful to portray himself as a man of virile, robust health. He shaved his head so no one could see that his hair was turning grey and avoided wearing spectacles in public. He also let it be known that he thought pyjamas were 'effete' and that he always slept in his underwear. Secretly, he suffered from a variety of health problems, including a crippling gastric ulcer which caused him to roll on the carpet in agony. He lived mostly on milk, drinking up to three litres a day to subdue his dreadful stomach ache. When he met Hitler he was careful to eat alone so as not to reveal his strange diet – he thought it would seem a bit 'unfascist'. Although Mussolini's doctors were generally reticent in their public pronouncements, Dr Aldo Castellani, an expert in tropical diseases, revealed that Mussolini in fact suffered from intestinal worms. According to Castellani, the roundworm that eventually emerged from an unspecified orifice of Il Duce was enormous – 'a real hyper-trophic fascist ascaris'.

The Dominican president Joseph Balaguer, who was said to be a deeply religious bachelor, wore black suits, black hats and black ties every day for nineteen years after his mother died in 1973 aged ninety-seven. Although he never married, Balaguer employed two female dwarfs as servants, by whom he fathered seven illegitimate children. During his 1994 election campaign he tried to win over women supporters by handing out red panties.

The least famous of Europe's great wartime dictators, General Franco, president of Spain, was not the most charismatic of leaders. Hitler once described meeting him as 'less pleasurable than having four or five teeth pulled'.

Stalin banned jazz. Hitler banned Mendelssohn because he was Jewish but revered Richard Wagner as an artistic god. Chairman Mao banned everything except his wife's operas. The Malawian dictator Dr Hastings Banda banned the song

'Delilah' made famous by the Welsh singer Tom Jones, in deference to a favourite mistress of the same name.

The Nazis were subject to intense Allied propaganda about their private lives, orchestrated by a secret department deep within the British Foreign Office, which was tasked to feed sex smears to the women of Germany in an attempt to destroy morale and destabilize the enemy. The supposed sexual peccadilloes of the most senior Nazis were contained in Foreign-Office files marked 'Retain or Destroy' and headed 'Adults Only'. The files alleged that Hitler's SS chief Heinrich Himmler was head of a cult that routinely indulged in group sex, egged on by the 'encouraging chanting' of the high priestess Ursula Deinert of the Berlin state opera. Other propaganda leaflets told of wife-swapping parties in Munich, where naked girls on white horses gave spirited renderings of the 'Ride of the Valkyries'. There was even a Nazi update on 'spin the bottle', whereby a naked girl was strapped to a roulette wheel with Nazi leader Christian Weber acting as croupier. Inevitably, Hitler's sex life was the subject of the thickest Foreign-Office file of all, most of it contradictory. There were rumours that he was homosexual, encouraged by his political enemies within the Third Reich. Many of his closest Nazi Party confidantes were homosexual, including his deputy Rudolf Hess, known to some as 'Hitler's First Lady', and on whom the Soviet KGB kept a dossier, including details of his habit of painting his toenails red, filed under his supposed name in homosexual circles, 'Black Paula'. Hitler's failure to rise above the rank of lance-corporal, in spite of his heroism in the First World War which had earned him two Iron Crosses, was rumoured to be the penalty for a court martial on a charge of indecency with a senior officer. Another senior Nazi official alleged that Hitler's military record contained two convictions for pederasty. In any event, after Hitler came to power the details of his military record were destroyed by the Gestapo. Even allowing for the taint of Allied disinformation, the Führer's sex life was undeniably odd. German womanhood by and large found Hitler highly fanciable; his penetrating eyes and ranting speeches, it was said, drove female listeners at his rallies to orgasm. He had a couple of affairs with actresses, including the young German film star Renate Müller. She claimed that above all Hitler enjoyed lying on the floor while being savagely kicked. Hitler formed a peculiar relationship with his niece Angelika 'Geli' Raubal, nineteen years his junior and the daughter of his half-sister Angela. According to one source, Geli confided to a friend that 'Uncle Alf' liked her to squat over his face and defecate on his head. Geli was found dead in Hitler's apartment, officially a suicide, eight months before he became Chancellor. Hitler was also very prudish, allowing no talk about even mildly sexual matters in his presence. When he learned that he had shaken hands with a former prostitute who was marrying one of his generals, he was horrified and immediately took multiple baths. He ranted about 'filth' in all sorts of forms and devoted thirteen pages to syphilis in *Mein Kampf*, describing it as a 'Jewish disease' that was 'transmitted generationally, and destroyed races, nations, and ultimately mankind'. The Führer, however, displayed many of the symptoms of advanced syphilis, including encephalitis (inflammation of the brain), dizziness, neck pustules, chest pain and an accentuated heartbeat. According to some sources he caught syphilis from a Jewish prostitute in Vienna around 1908; other accounts suggest he was given the diagnosis at a German field hospital in 1918, when he was recovering from a gas attack. Heinrich Himmler, the SS chief, saw to it that all his army medical records were destroyed. Eva Braun, who spent her last ten years with Hitler, confided to friends that their famous affair was completely sexless. Her diary entries on the subject of their sex life were obscure: in one she noted obliquely, 'He needs me for special reasons.' Fellow Nazi Ernst 'Putzi' Hanfstängl, a personal friend of Hitler's in the early years, believed that the Führer was repressed, and doubted that he ever experienced orthodox sexual relations with any woman. A leading British spy concurred, describing Eva Braun's relations with Hitler as 'of a platonic nature'. Testimonies of the Führer's lovers all agreed on one thing – his repellent body odour, the result of chronic flatulence.

Chairman Mao acquired an epic personal hygiene problem that grew steadily worse with old age. He never took a bath, although he did allow his servants to wipe him down every so often with a wet towel. During the Chinese Civil War in 1947, his doctor reproached him for using the same towel to dry both his face and feet. Mao refused to buy another one, saying, 'If every soldier refrains from buying a second towel, we shall be able to stage a second great campaign.' Mao scorned toothbrushes on the basis that 'tigers never brush their teeth', preferring to rinse his mouth out with tea once every morning. His teeth became covered with a heavy green film before they eventually turned black and fell out. In his later years he found eating so painful that he lived on stewed bamboo and stir-fried lettuce.

Hitler enjoyed reading pulp fiction. His favourite author was Karl May, a German writer of cheap American-style westerns. During the war Hitler admonished his generals for their 'lack of imagination', and recommended they all read Karl May.

Mussolini was renowned for sartorial eccentricity. When the King of Italy summoned him to form a government, Il Duce arrived wearing a black shirt, jodhpurs, spats and a bowler hat. Realizing that his attire was probably slightly outré for an audience with royalty, Mussolini excused himself by explaining, 'I have just come from the front.' In fact he had just come from his office. He stopped wearing bowler hats in 1930 when he found out that people were likening him to Oliver Hardy.

Stalin kept a secret stash of American films, mostly Tarzans and westerns, for his private viewing pleasure, commanding the presence of a translator. The translator was so terrified of saying the wrong thing that he avoided directly translating anything and stuck to describing the visual action that Stalin could see for himself. 'Uncle Joe' also loved a good politically correct home-grown musical. Among his favourite Soviet songfests were *Tractor Drivers*, *The Swineherd and the Shepherd* and *Hard Work, Happy Holiday*, featuring joyous harvest crews of dancing girls in overalls singing 'the quota has been attained' and 'our love blossoms like the wheat'. He saw his favourite Russian film *Volga, Volga* (1938) more than one hundred times, and even offered a copy to President Franklin D. Roosevelt. Stalin's favourite actress was Lyubov Orlova, wife of the film director Grigori Aleksandrov. When he met Orlova at the film studios he was surprised by how thin she was. 'Doesn't your husband feed you?' he asked, '. . . then we'll shoot him.' He was joking, for once. In 1934 Grigori Aleksandrov's *The Jolly Fellows* was banned by the Soviet film censors because it was ideologically unsound, but Stalin liked the film and had the ban lifted. 'Anyone who made a movie as funny as this one,' Stalin told Aleksandrov, 'has to be a brave man.' Stalin's film censor Ivan Bolshakov, head of the Central Film Industry Directorate, lived with the knowledge that his two cinematic predecessors had been shot. Once asked by a film-maker for an opinion of his work before Stalin had seen it, Bolshakov shrugged, saying, 'I don't know what I think of it yet.'

Hitler was delighted at his Christmas present from Goebbels in 1937 – fifteen Mickey Mouse cartoon films. Four years later, however, he declared Mickey an enemy of the Third Reich and banned him in Germany.

For much of his life Chairman Mao had something on his mind other than the struggle for proletarian leadership of the democratic revolution. Mao was obsessed with the notion that he could achieve longevity by increasing his number of sexual partners. Communist Party workers discovered that the way to keep their leader happy was with a permanent supply of nubile young females from politically correct peasant stock. At the height of the Cultural Revolution, Mao was often to be found in bed with three, four or even five young female volunteers simultaneously. Mao's sexual appetite, if not always his performance, increased with age. Well into his seventies he was still shedding his drab military uniform to bed several young women at a time. Temporary bouts of impotence were variously treated by doctors with injections of ground deer antlers and a secret formula called H3. Mao frequently suffered from venereal disease, but refused any treatment or to abstain from sex until the infection cleared. The young girls he regularly slept with considered catching VD from their Chairman to be a badge of honour, and proof of their close personal relationships to him.

When police searched the home of deposed Idi Amin in 1979, they found a large case full of old film reels of *I Love Lucy* and *Tom and Jerry* cartoons.

The private life of Romania's Royal Dictator King Carol II was the subject of much fantastic and lurid speculation. A sexual compulsive, he fed his addiction by sleeping with thousands of women and, it was alleged, created the post of full-time court abortionist to keep pace with his impregnations. It was said that the king was so abnormally well endowed that sex proved fatal for several of his mistresses, and a slush fund was set up to silence their families. According to another rumour, he had operations performed on his mistresses so that they were able to accommodate him sexually.

Mussolini's high-octane sex life was a key part of the appeal of the Italian fascist movement. Married with five children,

Il Duce had a string of mistresses and illegitimate offspring. He liked his women plump and had sex with them where he could, on the edge of his office desk or up against a wall, and always with his boots on. He claimed he had received a grenade wound in the First World War, which was almost certainly a lie to conceal a dose of syphilis caught in 1907 from an older married woman. Mussolini was so relieved to receive a doctor's report stating that he was finally clear of infection after fifteen years of treatment that he thought about sharing his good news by making the report public, but his political advisers talked him out of it.

Mussolini and Hitler both had ailurophobia – an aversion to cats.

The Libyan leader Colonel Muammar Gaddafi, famous for his marathon speeches, colourful designer robes and gun-toting female bodyguards dressed in figure-hugging combat gear, is routinely described in the Western press as 'eccentric'. In his autobiography *Fighting for Peace*, former US Defence Secretary Casper Weinberger noted: 'Rumours had long circulated in intelligence circles that Gaddafi suffered from an incurable venereal disease, and that this accounted for his occasional bouts of madness, in which hysteria, braggadocio and extreme theatricalism were all mixed.' The CIA, meanwhile, is in no doubt, claiming ownership of a lengthy dossier of detailed files proving that Gaddafi is impotent, insane and a cross-dresser; according to a CIA report filed in 1985, Gaddafi once made a trip to Majorca wearing make-up and carrying a teddy bear.

The North Korean dictator Kim Jong Il owns more than 20,000 videos, although his taste in films is less than revolutionary. Among his collection is a large library of western classics, specializing in John Wayne films, plus a comprehensive collection of Daffy Duck cartoons. One of his favourite films is said to be *The Godfather* – coincidentally, also the favourite movie of fellow 'Axis of Evil' member Saddam Hussein. Kim Jong Il has a full set of James Bond films. When he saw *Die Another Day*, in which the villain is the insane, power-mad son of a North Korean dictator, he became so agitated that he stabbed his Minister of Culture with a ballpoint pen and spat at the screen. While Kim can see any film he chooses, his countrymen are not quite so fortunate, and are fed a diet of propaganda about thermal power plants, or yet more propaganda about the Kim family. The biggest box-office hit in North Korea is *Sea of Blood*, a 'war musical' depicting Kim Jong Il's father – the former president Kim Il Sung – with some artistic licence, as a heroic guerrilla leader taking most of the credit for victories over Japan in the 1930s. It also features a hit song, 'My Heart Will Remain Faithful'.

Stalin lived a nocturnal existence and had a habit of phoning people in the middle of the night. On one such occasion he called the head of the State Broadcasting House to enquire about a Mozart piano concerto he had heard on the radio; who was the pianist and could he get a recording of it? The radio chief broke into a cold sweat, as no such recording existed. But how could he tell Stalin? There was no alternative but to summon all the members of the orchestra and the pianist to the recording studio in the middle of the night and make a recording of the concerto, to be delivered to Stalin in the morning. This record was still on the turntable when Stalin died.

Hitler was considered a crashing bore by most who kept company with him, regularly treating his sycophants to hours-long monologues. At a dinner party he once entertained fellow guests by marching up and down the room imitating different sorts of artillery fire.

Saddam's favourite film *The Godfather* was a huge influence on his management style. He had at least fifty-three of his relatives killed, including two sons-in-law, the Kamel brothers. In August 1995, following a fallout with Saddam's son Uday, the brothers defected to Jordan taking their wives with them. After telling the CIA everything they knew about Iraq's weapons programme, the brothers became homesick and, incredibly, accepted an undertaking from their father-in-law that they would come to no harm if they returned. Saddam asked Hussein Kamel, taking a line almost directly from the mouth of Michael Corleone, 'Would I kill the father of my grandchildren?' Saddam had them shot immediately upon their return.

Mussolini was convinced that Italy's lack of fighting spirit was down to eating pasta. The Roman legions, Il Duce reasoned, had survived on a diet of stodgy barley porridge and conquered the known world, while his own soldiers struggled even to defeat Albania on a diet of spaghetti. According to the fascist leader, flaccid tagliatelle was symbolic of the Italian male's lost virility.

Hitler became a vegetarian in 1931 when his doctors put him on a meatless diet to cure him of flatulence and a chronic stomach disorder, but he often lapsed; according to his cook, he was partial to sausages and stuffed pigeon. He spent his final hours gorging himself on chocolate cake.

The Libyan leader Colonel Muammar Gaddafi regularly flies planeloads of camels to international conferences, then parks them on the hotel lawns – all so that he can enjoy their milk.

The favourite dish of North Korea's Dear Leader Kim Jong Il is roast donkey eaten with silver chopsticks. In North Korea this delicacy is known as 'celestial cow', out of respect to Kim Jong Il's late father, Kim Il Sung, who did not eat donkey.

Stalin's bad-tempered paranoia was exacerbated by badly-fitting false teeth and sore gums. He was quite fond of bananas, one of the few foods he could enjoy without discomfort. A Politburo member once presented Stalin with a crate of bananas which, to Uncle Joe's fury, were discovered to be underripe. Stalin immediately sacked his Trade Minister and had the ship's captain responsible for importing the bananas arrested.

Idi Amin was a cannibal, albeit a reluctant one: he said he found human flesh 'too salty'.

Both Stalin and Chairman Mao chain-smoked cigarettes (when Mao's doctor asked him to cut down on his lifelong three-pack-a-day habit he countered, 'Smoking is also a form of deep-breathing exercise, don't you think?') unlike Hitler, who called tobacco 'the wrath of the red man against the white man, vengeance for having been given hard liquor'. Adolf attributed his personal success to non-smoking, claiming in 1942: 'I am convinced that if I had been a smoker, I never would have been able to bear the cares and anxieties which have been a burden to me for so long. Perhaps the German people owe their salvation to that fact.' He banned smoking in his bunker and gave gold watches to associates who kicked the habit; it didn't stop them lighting up the moment they heard the Führer had committed suicide, however.

Thousands of bottles of Hennessy Paradis are shipped to North Korea for the personal consumption of Kim Jong Il every year, confirming the Dear Leader as the world's biggest buyer of the French cognac, with an estimated annual account of £400,000 to £600,000 since 1992. Kim's annual spend on cognac – which costs £400 a bottle in Seoul – is 770 times the income of the average North Korean citizen.

According to one of Idi Amin's surviving physicians, 'Big Daddy' was administered treatment for tertiary syphilis. In 1974 Amin lectured students at Kampala's conference centre: 'I am told venereal disease is very high with you. You had better go to hospital and make yourselves very clean, or you will infect the whole population.'

Adolf Hitler had a half-brother, Alois, and a sister-in-law, Bridget, who lived in Liverpool. Bridget Hitler tried to cash in on her family connection by writing a book, *My Brother-in-Law Adolf*, but couldn't find a publisher. The most contentious claim in the 225-page typescript was that Adolf spent six months with them at their flat at 102 Upper Stanhope Street from November 1912. Hitler never once mentioned his visit to England, according to Bridget, because he was avoiding compulsory service in the Austrian army. The trip, however, made a lasting impression on the Führer. Before adopting his famous toothbrush moustache, Hitler experimented with a variety of facial hairstyles from a 'full set' to a pointed goatee; at the time of his trip to England he was sporting a large handlebar moustache. Before he took leave of his sister-in-law in May 1913, Bridget advised him to trim it. Years later, when she saw his picture in a newspaper, she knew that he had taken her advice, but noted in her book: 'Adolf had gone too far.'

The Dominican strongman Rafael Trujillo, who developed an obsession with clothing and perfume, collected neckties; he owned more than 10,000 upon his death.

During the reign of Enver Hoxha, the only Western films shown in Albania were those starring the English comedian Norman Wisdom – or 'Pitkin', as he was known to his Albanian fans. No one can be sure why Wisdom's films alone escaped censorship; it may have been that Hoxha considered them ideologically sound – that the downtrodden Norman Pitkin's struggles against the decadent Mr Grimsdale in such films as *Pitkini Ne Dyqan* (*Pitkin at the Store*) and *Pitkini Ne Spital* (*Pitkin in the Hospital*) were a communist parable on the class war, showing a member of the oppressed proletariat triumphing against capitalism. Or it could have been that the plot lines were just so silly that even Hoxha's legendary paranoia was not alerted. In any event, as the country's only permitted Western film star, Norman Wisdom became Albania's second biggest national folk hero after Mother Teresa.

Adolf Hitler once attempted to cure his chronic flatulence by drinking machine-gun oil.

PROFILE: JOSEF STALIN

Born: Iosif Vissarionovich Dzhugashvili on 21 December 1879.

Died: 5 March 1953.

Also known as: Koba; 'Uncle Joe'.

Occupation: Premier of the Soviet Union 1941–53.

Hobbies: Gardening, poetry, playing billiards and cinema: he saw his favourite film, the 1938 *Boys Town* starring Spencer Tracy, at least twenty-five times.

Career highlight: In a single day in December 1938, 'Uncle Joe' signed 3,182 death warrants.

Career lowlight: Left to die in a puddle of urine on the floor by attendants, who were too afraid to enter his bedroom uninvited.

Significant others: Wives Kato and Nadya.

Family: Sons Yakov and Vasily, and daughter Svetlana.

Style: Big boots, big moustaches, superhero-like statuary, extreme paranoia.

Whimsical cruelty factor:

Had prisoners beaten so hard that their eyeballs literally popped out; deaths during interrogation were always registered as heart attacks.

Legacy: He caused the death of about 30 million of his comrades through war, famine, exile and execution – more than Ivan the Terrible and all of the other Russian Tsars combined managed in over four centuries.

Wit and wisdom: 'The death of a man is a tragedy: the death of a thousand is a statistic.'

PROFILE: MUAMMAR GADDAFI

Born: 1942 (the precise date is unknown).

Also known as: 'Brother General'; 'the Mad Dog' (this latter moniker was coined by Ronald Reagan, the fortieth US President). There are at least thirty-two different ways to spell his surname in English including Kazzafi, Gadafy, Gadhafi, Gheddafi, Qadhdhaafi. The name derives from an Arabic verb meaning to fling, hurl, toss, push, shove, pelt, eject, oust, defame, slander, strafe or vomit.

Occupation: President of Libya 1969–present (at time of writing); (full title 'Colonel Muammar Abu Minyal al Gaddafi, Leader of the Revolution').

Hobbies: Throwing money at crowds from his car window; surfing the Internet.

Career highlight: His interview with John Simpson of the BBC. Gaddafi donned a straw, trilby-style hat worn sideways for the occasion. When Simpson's cameraman played back the interview tape, the microphone clipped to the leader's chest had picked up repeated farting.

Career lowlights: Lockerbie, the UTA airliner bombing, the shooting of PC Yvonne Fletcher in London, the Berlin disco bombing, supplying arms to the IRA.

Significant others: The 'Gaddafi girls' – his unique, personal bodyguard of young Libyan females, who sport figure-hugging combat gear and hardened fingernails an inch long, coated in a deep purple gloss which looks like congealed blood.

Style: Ageing rock star; fond of purple and gold designer robes that he has been known to change five times in one day; T-shirts screen-printed with photographs of African leaders.

Whimsical cruelty factor:

According to one victim, confessions are routinely extracted by torture methods 'of all types known since the Middle Ages'.

Legacy: Various internal assassinations, 'disappearances' and human-rights abuses.

Wit and wisdom: 'American soldiers must be turned into lambs – and eating them is tolerated.'

CHAPTER 9
Dead Dictators

Paraguay's paranoid Perpetual Dictator Jose Francia, known informally as *El Supremo*, did not allow anyone in his presence to stand within six paces and only then with their hands well away from their sides. At the age of seventy-nine Francia took to his bed with a chill. A physician was called to examine him, but when he strayed within the permitted distance Francia stabbed him with a sabre. Untended, the dictator died the following day.

Lenin has been a poor conversationalist since 1924, but the world's most famous embalmed man has still managed to get through several dozen new suits. Under his blue acrylic tailored three-piece, the father of Russian Communism also wears a rubber wetsuit into which is poured the solution that keeps him from falling apart. Twice a week the parts that are visible (his hands and face) are painted with fresh embalming fluid and every eighteen months the whole body is lifted out and given a thoroughly good soaking. Every four years a bit of Lenin is scraped off, placed under a microscope and examined for signs of deterioration. About 60 per cent of his body is now made of wax, including his ears. He is also said to have a growth of fungus around his neck and on the back of his head that wasn't there when he led the Bolsheviks to power in 1917. Lenin continues to be a crowd-puller in Moscow, even though neither his reputation nor the queues are quite what they were. When communism was still popular, Lenin had an air-conditioning unit fitted inside his chest to stop his body parts melting from the body heat of visiting tourists.

Adolf Hitler's charred remains were positively identified by his teeth, which were discovered by Soviet soldiers in a shallow grave outside his Berlin bunker in 1945, and since locked away in an archive in Moscow. The post-mortem performed by Russian doctors on Hitler's body confirmed the music-hall joke that he had indeed only one ball, although it has never been determined whether he was born deformed or, as some medical historians believe, the missing gonad had been removed surgically – possibly as a result of a bullet in the groin during the First World War, or as common practice when advanced syphilis reaches the potentially fatal stage. There was, however, another version of events from the person who was perhaps best placed to know the truth. According to Eva Braun, Hitler's testicular damage was the result of a boyhood mishap with a wild alpine goat.

The hardline anti-communist Rafael Trujillo was a convicted rapist, a minor detail overlooked by the Dominican dictator's friends in the American government. US Secretary of State Cordell Hull was fond of saying, 'He may be a son of a bitch, but he is our son of a bitch'; a sentiment he expressed about both Trujillo and the Nicaraguan dictator Anastasio Somoza. In 1961, however, relations between Trujillo and the White House became strained when the despot tried to retire his neighbour, the Venezuelan President Romulo Betancourt, with a large bomb. The Eisenhower administration did a swift U-turn and approved a CIA plan to remove their old ally. On 30 May 1961, as Trujillo and his chauffeur were driving unescorted along a quiet country road, they were ambushed by two carloads of armed gunmen. The sixty-nine-year-old dictator stepped out of his car and tried to bluff his way out of impending death, but was shot twenty-nine times at point-blank range, his body run over, tossed into the boot of another car, then dumped by the roadside on Santa Domingo's George Washington Avenue. All but two of the conspirators met a violent end at the hands of the vengeful Trujillo family and, in most cases, one more gruesome than that of their victim. One conspirator was fed the flesh of his own son, then presented with his son's head on a plate; the father had a fatal heart attack.

Seventy-four-year-old Josef Stalin was about to launch his biggest leadership purge yet, when he was felled by a fatal stroke and lay helpless on the floor in a pool of his own urine, unable to call for help. As no one dared to go into his rooms uninvited, it was hours before his bodyguards finally summoned up the courage to open his door, which gave Stalin plenty of time to reflect upon the fact that he had recently ordered the arrest and torture of his family doctor. A maid finally sent for Stalin's highest ranking subordinate Lavrenti Beria, who took the curious decision to shut the door and leave his leader 'undiscovered' until the following morning – enough time for Beria to search through Stalin's safe and files for incriminating documents, including evidence against himself. When medical help finally arrived the terrified doctors were reluctant at first even to touch Stalin to take his pulse, however leeches were applied to his ears and he was administered enemas of magnesium sulphate and spoonfuls of weak tea. He died five days later. A few months later, Stalin's former right-hand man was dramatically arrested and tried on thirty-nine counts of sexual assault; a search of Beria's office had revealed a large stash of female underwear. As neither his responsibility for mass murder in the Stalin era nor his own record as a multiple rapist could be publicly mentioned for fear of bringing the Communist regime into disrepute, Beria was declared guilty of a plot 'to revive capitalism' and summarily executed, his name wiped from public memory. In true Stalinist tradition, subscribers to the Great Soviet Encyclopaedia were advised to use 'a small knife or razor blade' to remove the entry on Beria and then to insert a replacement article on the Bering Sea.

Enver Hoxha instructed his wife Nexhmije to build a pyramid after his death to house everything he owned. The huge, white, marble and glass Enver Hoxha Memorial Museum was duly stocked with the collected artefacts of the late dictator, including such vital state treasures as some of his old toiletries. After the fall of communism in Albania, the museum became a disco.

In 1968 a toilet seat allegedly belonging to Adolf Hitler was put up for auction in Los Angeles, California. The seller, former US fighter pilot Guy Harris, claimed he had rescued it from Hitler's bunker in 1945 – the only item he could find that had not already been scavenged by Russian troops.

The biggest museum in Paraguay, the Museum of Military History, has an entire room given over to the late dictator Francisco Solano Lopez. Highlights include a display of his pyjamas and a pair of giant-sized underpants.

North Korea is the only country in the world ruled by a corpse. President Kim Il Sung died in July 1994 from a massive heart attack during an animated argument with his son, Kim Jong Il. North Korea observed a 100-day period of mourning, after which the recently deceased dictator was rechristened Eternal Leader. The 'immortal and imperishable' late Kim Il Sung is currently resting in a glass coffin in a giant mausoleum, the Kumsusan Memorial Palace, where his skin is tweaked and powdered by Russian embalming experts once a month.

After a decade of bizarre and brutal dictatorship Macias Nguema, ruler of Equatorial Guinea, was overthrown in 1979 by his nephew Teodor, who unflatteringly dismissed his uncle as 'an envoy of the devil and president of sorcerers'. Nguema was tried for genocide, treason and embezzlement and sentenced to death. The firing squad had to be imported from

Morocco because local troops refused to shoot their former boss. They said that Nguema's spirit was too strong for mere bullets and that he would undoubtedly return as a tiger.

Infirm for the last five years of his life, Chairman Mao finally succumbed to a fatal neurological disorder in 1976. Although Mao had requested cremation, his immediate successor Hua Guofeng overruled him; the late Chinese leader was to be preserved for all time. It was a nigh impossible task, given the primitive state of Chinese embalming technology. The decision also came far too late, as Mao's vital organs should have been removed, and the arteries and veins flushed out, within two hours of death. To complicate matters further, the task of mummification fell to Mao's personal physician, Dr Li Zhisui, a complete novice at embalming corpses. To keep the body in reasonable shape until the memorial service, Li pumped about 40 litres of formaldehyde into Mao's corpse – almost twice the advised limit. Mao's head was so full of embalming fluid that it made his ears stick out at right angles, although this still did not prevent his nose from falling off four weeks later. Mao is now apparently shrinking at a steady rate of about 5 per cent a year. The official line given by the mausoleum director is that this is merely an optical illusion caused by the curious lighting effects in the hall which contains his corpse; according to legend, however, Mao has long since been replaced by a wax dummy.

Cambodian dictator Pol Pot died peacefully in his sleep in April 1998, evading prosecution for the deaths of as many as 2 million of his countrymen. He was seventy-three.

Benito Mussolini tried to escape the advancing Allied army but was found hiding in the back of a truck heading for the Alps wearing a private's overcoat over his striped general's pants. He and his long-standing mistress Clara Petacci were executed on the spot by machine-gun fire, then taken to a Milan square, the Piazzale Loreto, and strung up by their feet with piano wire from the girders of a petrol station. Petacci's skirt was discreetly tied about her legs with the belt of a chivalrous partisan. An immense crowd spat at, kicked and even pumped more bullets into the exposed corpses. A year later Mussolini's body vanished from its supposedly secret, unmarked grave in a municipal cemetery. The bodysnatchers were fascists intent on a publicity stunt; Mussolini's corpse was now a symbol of the old order for those nostalgic for his regime. A message left in the grave read: 'Finally, O Duce, you are with us. We will cover you with roses, but the smell of your virtue will overpower those roses.' Four months later, what remained of Il Duce was found in a small trunk just outside Milan and two Franciscan monks were charged with hiding his body. It emerged that in the intervening months, the corpse had been kept on the move, variously hidden in a villa, a monastery and a convent. Il Duce was buried a second time in an undisclosed location, only to be dug up yet again eleven years later and returned to his widow Rachele, who buried him again in Predappio in 1957. Mussolini's brain, however, had been removed and shipped to the United States in 1945 for scientific experimentation, to see if it shed any light on the human condition: it didn't.

The most courageous American mail-order con of all time began in 1946, a year after Hitler's death, and lasted for a decade. William Johnson, a semi-literate miner from Kentucky, decided to cash in on a rumour sweeping America that Hitler had been smuggled out of Europe after the Second World War and was alive and well and living in North America. Johnson, posing as Hitler, now 'settled in Kentucky with some of his Nazi chiefs of staff, and planning to take over the United States', made a public appeal for cash to help his cause. It generated a steady stream of postal orders for the best part of a decade, from right-wing Americans and fascists of German extraction, to help fund his dastardly plans for space ships, 'invisible ships' and underground hordes of ammunition. The American public sent him tens of thousands of dollars, even though Johnson often signed his name as 'The Furrier' instead of 'The Führer'.

'Papa Doc' Duvalier made all of his most important decisions on the 22nd of the month, his 'lucky day' on which he believed he was guarded by his voodoo spirits. He placed a curse on US President John F. Kennedy and was delighted when JFK was assassinated on 22 November 1963, a coincidence that greatly enhanced the reputation of his alleged voodoo powers. Papa Doc claimed he could predict the future from his late-night conversations with a severed human head, which he kept in a cupboard in the presidential palace. It belonged to one of his former army officers Blucher Philogenes, who had led a doomed CIA-backed invasion of Haiti in 1963. In later years Papa Doc only ever dared leave his presidential palace on the 22nd of the month. Although he liked to compare himself to the undead, Papa Doc stayed dead after succumbing to fatal diabetes in April 1971. The announcement of his death was made on 22 April, although he had been dead for several days by then.

In 1983 the German magazine *Stern* paid £2.3 million (about £50 a word) for 'the publishing scoop of the century', sixty-two volumes of Adolf Hitler's diaries dated from 1932 to 1945, covering the complete Third Reich. The remarkable volumes, *Stern* reported, had been found by farmers in a plane crash at the end of the war, and had eventually made their way into the hands of *Stern*'s investigative reporter, Gerd 'the Detective' Heidemann. Suspiciously, the diaries shed little light on the momentous events of the age and were mostly a collection of banal personal musings; a typical excerpt dated June 1935 read: 'Eva now has two dogs, so she won't get bored.' An entry from December 1938 revealed: 'Now a year is nearly over. Have I achieved my goals for the Reich? Save for a few small details, yes!' Another during the 1936 Berlin Olympics read: 'Eva wants to come to the Games in Berlin, have had tickets delivered to her and her girlfriends. Hope my flatulence doesn't return during the Games.' Voices of scepticism were raised. Hitler, it was pointed out, notoriously hated taking notes. The diary covers were also decorated with the brass Gothic initials 'FH', the author having apparently mistaken the Gothic capital 'F' for an 'A' when he bought the type. Nevertheless, the diaries were vouched as genuine by the great and much respected English historian Hugh Trevor-Roper, who declared, 'I'm staking my reputation on it.' A few months later they were exposed as a clumsy modern forgery, written in the back room of a Stuttgart shop by Konrad Kujau, a small-time dealer in Nazi memorabilia. Herr Kujau's earlier creations included a sequel to *Mein Kampf*, poems by Adolf Hitler and the beginnings of an opera penned by the Führer entitled *Wieland der Schmied* (*Wieland the Blacksmith*).

The fall of Nicolae and Elena Ceausescu was the first revolution to be shown live on TV. In December 1989 Ceausescu tried to address a mass rally in front of the Central Committee building in Bucharest, to show the world that the workers of Romania still loved him. By the time of this, his final public speech, enthusiasm for 'the Most Loved and Esteemed Son and Daughter of the Romanian People' had dwindled so much that the applause had to be taped. For the first time in his career Ceausescu was rudely interrupted in mid-sentence by shouts of disapproval. Egged on by his wife he tried to finish his speech but then, as the tape with pre-recorded applause and cheers was abruptly switched off, he decided to make a run for it. The presidential couple were captured attempting to flee the capital by helicopter. They were quickly tried and convicted by a military tribunal on charges of mass murder and theft, and executed by a firing squad on Christmas Day, the soldiers firing so enthusiastically that they accidentally shot each other. The freshly bleeding corpses of Nicolae and Elena were shown on TV as proof that their reign was over, then they were wrapped in tent cloth, bundled aboard a waiting helicopter and dropped in the middle of a sports stadium in a Bucharest suburb. The following morning, to all-round embarrassment, the corpses went missing. They turned up later in a nearby shed. Nicolae Ceausescu's honorary knighthood, awarded to him during his visit to Britain in 1978, had been revoked only hours before his execution.

The Marxist dictator Ali Soilih escaped numerous attempts on his life and four unsuccessful coups during his two-and-a-half-year reign in the Comoros, a tiny Indian Ocean island group just north-west of Madagascar, in the mid-1970s. Soilih wanted to return the Comoros to 'Year Zero' by burning government records, banning traditional weddings and funerals, legalizing marijuana and placing teenagers in high government offices. He lowered the voting age to fourteen, appointed a fifteen-year-old to run the police department and mobilized Comoran youth into a special revolutionary militia, which launched violent Red Guard-style attacks on their elders. On 13 May 1978 he was finally overthrown in a coup led by an infamous French mercenary, 'Colonel Bob' Denard, who landed in the dead of night with forty-six men in a converted trawler. Denard found Soilih with his guard down, sharing his bed with three young girls while enjoying a pornographic film. Soilih was placed under house arrest and a few days later he was shot dead during a supposed 'rescue attempt'. His body was draped over the hood of Denard's jeep and dropped off at his mother's property for burial.

In 1987 the hands of the Argentinian president Juan Perón were amputated and were subject to a £5 million ransom demand. Fortunately Perón had no further use for them, as he had already been dead for thirteen years.

To the end, Idi Amin was known as 'Dr Jaffa', an affectionate title deriving from his excessive consumption of oranges; the former cannibal having turned fruitarian in his twilight years. One old habit remained to the last, however: he died with his favourite, ever-present portrait above his bed; that of a kilted King George VI or, as Amin used to call him, 'my old commander-in-chief'.

Stalin is the only twentieth-century dictator to have his own theme park. Stalin World, ninety miles south-west of Vilnius in Lithuania, is part amusement park, part open-air museum, circled by barbed wire and guard towers, and dotted with sixty-five bronze and granite statues of former Soviet leaders and assorted communist VIPs. During the facility's gala opening in April 2001, thousands of invited guests were greeted at the gate by an actor dressed as Stalin, while a Lenin lookalike, complete with false goatee beard, tweed jacket and cap, sat fishing at a nearby pond. Visitors were also invited to drink shots of vodka and eat cold borscht soup from tin bowls at the Gulag restaurant, while loud speakers blared old communist hymns. The hopeful owner, mushroom magnate Viliumas Malinauskas, said he got the idea after winning a competition held to get rid of a batch of statues of communist heroes that were torn down with the fall of the Soviet Union in 1991. He explained to assembled journalists: 'It combines the charms of a Disneyland with the worst of the Soviet gulag prison camp.'

Severe illness forced Spanish dictator General Franco to resign in 1973, but he lingered on much longer than even his doctors or his supporters anticipated. On his deathbed at last, two years later, Franco was told that General Garcia wished to say goodbye. 'Why?' Franco enquired. 'Is Garcia going somewhere?'

PROFILE:
ADOLF HITLER

Born: 20 April 1889 at Braunau-am-Inn, Austria.

Died: 30 April 1945 in Berlin, Germany.

Also known as: Der Führer; Wolf; Carpet Biter.

Occupation: Chancellor of Germany 1933–45.

Hobbies: Painting and travel.

Career highlight: Voted *Time* magazine's 'Man Of The Year' in 1938.

Career lowlight: Two rejections from the Viennese Academy of Fine Arts: he blamed it on the Jewish members of the review board, not lack of talent.

Significant others: Wife Eva Braun.

Style: Brown shirts and toothbrush moustaches.

Whimsical cruelty factor: 👢👢

Tendency to order executions when depressed; preferred dogs to people, but still tested a fatal dose of prussic acid on his much-loved Alsatian Blondi.

Legacy: Fifty million dead; the VW Beetle.

Wit and wisdom: 'Anyone who sees and paints a sky green and fields blue ought to be sterilized.'

PROFILE: POL POT

Born: Solath Sar on 19 May 1925.

Died: 15 April 1998.

Also known as: Brother Number One.

Occupation: Prime Minister of Cambodia 1975–9.

Career highlight: After leading the Khmer Rouge guerrilla forces to victory in 1975, declared 'Year Zero', a radical attempt to create a communist utopia; infringements punishable by death included not working hard enough, complaining about living conditions, stealing food, wearing jewellery, engaging in sexual relations, grieving over the loss of relatives or friends, expressing religious sentiments, knowing a foreign language and wearing glasses.

Career lowlight: Living in the jungle on the run from the police, plagued with gastric problems and, suspecting he was being poisoned, surviving by eating lizards.

Significant others: First wife Khieu Ponnary, also known as 'Sister Number One'; when she went mad in the late 1970s he had her committed to a mental institution and took a much younger second wife, Mea Som.

Style: Grey Mao suits or black pyjamas, the working attire of the Khmer Rouge.

Whimsical cruelty factor: 🐦 🐦 🐦 🐦 🐦

Executed people with stone axes to save on bullets.

Legacy: About 2 million dead – between a quarter and a third of his country's population – through imprisonment, torture, overwork, starvation and execution; the 'killing fields'.

APPENDIX I
Auto-crats

Hitler never drove, but he was the driving force behind the development of Professor Porsche's KdF-wagen – the 'Strength Through Joy' car, or Volkswagen Beetle as it came to be known. He sketched the original Beetle design on a napkin at a restaurant table in Munich in 1932. Hitler preferred to be driven along his new autobahnen in a big, powerful, bomb-proof Mercedes-Benz. His preference was for eight-cylinder open-topped models, such as the six-wheeled Mercedes G-4, so the German people could see his smartly pressed uniforms. Hitler was so proud of his country's automobile industry that in 1939, when Nazi Germany and the Soviet Union signed their pact of non-aggression, he gave a supercharged sports Mercedes roadster to his good friend, Joe Stalin.

The Soviet Union's home-grown ZIS – Zavod Imiena Stalina – was originally named after Stalin, but later renamed ZIL. Stalin's personal favourite, a special 1949 ZIS eight-cylinder limousine, was a 20-foot long, 7-ton behemoth with 3-inch-thick bulletproof glass. It did about 4 mph on a good run.

Stalin once presented Chairman Mao with five ZIS bullet-proof stretch limousines with art deco-style red flags on their crest. Mao was so impressed that he commissioned a home-made, 10-metre-long, luxury, six-door stretch 'Red Flag' limousine, complete with fridge, telephone, TV, double bed, desk and sofa. He died in 1976 before he could use it.

Hitler is often given the credit for inventing the motorway, but that honour goes to Benito Mussolini, who ordered the construction of the first *autostrada* tollway between Milan and the northern Italian lakes, completed in 1923. Germany's first autobahn was built between Cologne and Bonn in 1929, before Hitler came to power.

Lenin liked to travel in style; the father of the Russian revolution owned an excessive nine Rolls-Royces during his Soviet leadership. One, a Silver Ghost open tourer, is exhibited in the Lenin Museum of Moscow. His was not the first Rolls-Royce in Russia; Tsar Nicholas II had two Silver Ghosts, Josef Stalin also had a Roller, as did Leonid Brezhnev, part of his extensive car collection.

Among the revolutionary memorabilia on view in Tripoli museum, pride of place goes to a turquoise Volkswagen Beetle, circa 1967, registration number 23398 LB: the car that Colonel Gaddafi used while plotting his coup against the Libyan ruler King Idris in 1979.

'Papa Doc' Duvalier travelled in a Mercedes 600, throwing wads of banknotes out of the window as he went. The Mercedes stretch limo became so popular among African despots (President Mobutu of Zaire owned fifty-one of them) that the political elite are known in Swahili as 'wabenzi' – 'men of Mercedes-Benz'.

Because of his anti-Soviet stance, Nicolae Ceausescu was courted by the West and regularly showered with gifts by visiting dignitaries. These presents included several cars – a '75 Buick Electra 225 from his good friend US President Richard Nixon; a '74 Hillman from the Shah of Iran; and a customized '71 Volkswagen, a gift from the West German Chancellor – complete with gun-port facilities.

In 1991 the Libyan leader Colonel Gaddafi announced that he had invented the world's safest vehicle, a revolutionary 'Rocket car' featuring all-round air bags, an inbuilt electronic defence system and a collapsible front bumper to protect passengers in head-on collisions. A Libyan government official described the car as proof that Gaddafi was 'thinking of ways to preserve human life all over the world', and predicted that Libya would turn out 50,000 cars a year. Nothing more was ever heard of the 'Rocket'.

APPENDIX II
Former Occupations

1. Marshal Tito – locksmith
2. Josef Stalin – trainee priest, apprentice cobbler
3. Rafael Trujillo and General Ne Win – post-office clerks
4. Benito Mussolini and Mao Zedong – trainee teachers
5. 'Papa Doc' Duvalier – family doctor
6. Enver Hoxha – tobacconist
7. Ferdinand Marcos – criminal lawyer
8. Nicolae Ceausescu – shoemaker
9. Pol Pot – Buddhist monk
10. Idi Amin – doughnut vendor

APPENDIX III
Unsung Siblings

1. Paula Hitler – younger sister of Adolf
2. Arnaldo Mussolini – kid brother of Benito
3. Ilie Ceausescu – little brother of Nicolae
4. Mao Zemin – little brother of Mao Zedong
5. Hector Biembenido Trujillo – younger brother of Rafael
6. Marie-Denise Duvalier – big sister of Baby Doc
7. Saloth Neap – the not remotely genocidal brother of Pol Pot
8. Kim Kyong-hui – big sister of Kim Jong Il
9. Omm Omar Hussein – little sister of Saddam
10. Amule Amin Dada – big brother of Idi

APPENDIX IV
Silver Screen Despots

1. Charlie Chaplin – *The Great Dictator* (1940)
2. Jack Palance – Fidel Castro in *Che!* (1969)
3. Alec Guinness – *Hitler: The Last Ten Days* (1973)
4. Rod Steiger – *The Last Days of Mussolini* (1974)
5. Joseph Olita – *Amin: The Rise and Fall* (1982)
6. Robert Duvall – *Stalin* (1992)
7. Jonathan Pryce – Juan Perón in *Evita* (1996)
8. Claudio Spadaro – *Tea With Mussolini* (1999)
9. Bob Hoskins – Mussolini in *Mussolini: The Decline and Fall of Il Duce* (1985) and Manuel Noriega in *Noriega: God's Favorite* (2000)
10. Noah Taylor – Adolf Hitler in *Max* (2002)

APPENDIX V
Scintillating Sources

ALMOND, MARK
   The Rise and Fall of Nicolae and Elena Ceausescu
   (Chapmans Publishers, 1992)
AXELROD, ALAN and PHILLIPS, CHARLES
   *Dictators and Tyrants: Absolute Rulers and Would-Be Rulers
   in World History* (Facts on File Inc., 1995)
BULLOCK, ALAN
   Hitler and Stalin: Parallel Lives (Fontana Press, 1998)
CAWTHORNE, NIGEL
   The Empress of South America (Arrow, 2003)
DECALO, SAMUEL
   Psychoses of Power: African Personal Dictatorships
   (Westview Press, 1989)
DIEDERICH, BERNARD
   Papa Doc: Haiti and Its Dictator (Penguin Books, 1972)
DIEDERICH, BERNARD
   Trujillo: The Death of the Dictator
   (Markus Wiener Publishers, 2000)
FERGUSON, JAMES
   Papa Doc, Baby Doc (Blackwell Publishers, 1988)

GIMLETT, JOHN
    At the Tomb of the Inflatable Pig: Travels Through Paraguay
    (Arrow, 2004)
KAMAU, JOSEPH and CAMERON, ANDREW
    Lust to Kill: Rise and Fall of Idi Amin (Corgi Books, 1979)
KERSHAW, IAN
    Hitler, 1889–1936: Hubris (Penguin Books, 2001)
KERSHAW, IAN
    Hitler, 1936–1945: Nemesis (Penguin Books, 2001)
LI, ZHISUI et al
    The Private Life of Chairman Mao (Random House, 1996)
LLOSA, MARIO VARGAS
    The Feast of the Goat (Faber and Faber, 2003)
ORIZIO, RICCARDO
    Talk of the Devil: Encounters with Seven Dictators
    (Vintage, 2004)
PACEPA, ION MIHAI
    Red Horizons: The True Story of Nicolae and Elena
    Ceausescu's Crimes, Lifestyle and Corruption
    (Regnery Gateway, 1990)
SEBAG-MONTEFIORE, SIMON
    Stalin: The Court of the Red Tsar
    (Weidenfeld and Nicolson, 2003)
SMITH, DENIS MACK
    Mussolini (Weidenfeld and Nicolson, 2001)
SMITH, GEORGE IVAN
    Ghosts of Kampala: Rise and Fall of Idi Amin
    (HarperCollins, 1980)
WRONG, MICHELA
    In the Footsteps of Mr Kurtz: Living on the Brink of Disaster
    in Mobutu's Congo (Perennial, 2002)